BECOMING
A MEDIA
MENTOR

ALA Editions purchases fund advocacy, awareness, and accreditation programs for library professionals worldwide.

BECOMING A MEDIA MENTOR

A Guide for Working with Children and Families

CLAUDIA HAINES, CEN CAMPBELL
and the
ASSOCIATION FOR LIBRARY SERVICE TO CHILDREN (ALSC)

FOREWORD BY
CHIP DONOHUE

An imprint of the American Library Association

CHICAGO   2016

CLAUDIA HAINES leads storytimes, hosts maker programs, and gets great books into the hands of kids and teens as the youth services librarian and media mentor at the Homer (Alaska) Public Library. She is a coauthor of the Association for Library Service to Children's white paper, *Media Mentorship in Libraries Serving Youth,* and trains other librarians as media mentors. She serves on local and national committees that support families and literacy. She blogs at www.nevershushed.com.

CEN CAMPBELL is a children's librarian, an author, and the founder of LittleeLit.com. She has driven a bookmobile, managed branch libraries, and developed innovative programs for babies, young children, and teens, and now supports children's librarians who serve as media mentors in their communities. She was named a *Library Journal* Mover and Shaker in 2014 for her work on LittleeLit.com. She is a coauthor of the Association for Library Service to Children's white paper, *Media Mentorship in Libraries Serving Youth.*

© 2016 by the American Library Association

Extensive effort has gone into ensuring the reliability of the information in this book; however, the publisher makes no warranty, express or implied, with respect to the material contained herein.

ISBNs
978-0-8389-1463-2 (paper)
978-0-8389-1470-0 (PDF)
978-0-8389-1471-7 (ePub)
978-0-8389-1472-4 (Kindle)

Library of Congress Cataloging-in-Publication Data

Names: Haines, Claudia, author. | Campbell, Cen, author.| Association for Library Service to Children, author.
Title: Becoming a media mentor : a guide for working with children and families / Claudia Haines, Cen Campbell, and the Association for Library Service to Children.
Description: Chicago : ALA Editions, an imprint of the American Library Association, 2016. | Includes bibliographical references and index.
Identifiers: LCCN 2016013272| ISBN 9780838914632 (paperback) | ISBN 9780838914717 (ePub) | ISBN 9780838914700 (PDF) | ISBN 9780838914724 (Kindle)
Subjects: LCSH: Multimedia library services—United States. | Children's digital libraries—United States. | Media librarians—United States. | Digital media. | Application software. | Children's libraries—Activity programs. | Libraries and families. | Media literacy—Study and teaching. | Computer literacy—Study and teaching. | Electronic information resource literacy—Study and teaching.
Classification: LCC ZA4084.M85 C36 2016 | DDC 025.5/2—dc23 LC record available at https://lccn.loc.gov/2016013272

Cover design by Krista Joy Johnson; image © VectorState. Text composition by Dianne M. Rooney in the Chaparral, Gotham, and Bell Gothic typefaces.

⊗ This paper meets the requirements of ANSI/NISO Z39.48-1992 (Permanence of Paper).

Printed in the United States of America

20 19 18 17 16   5 4 3 2 1

To Owen and Olivia, my first reasons to be a media mentor,
and to Steve, who gave me the time and support to write
—Claudia

To Jude, whose existence made me think about media
and young children in the first place, and to Laszlo,
who joined us when this book was being written
—Cen

Contents

APPENDIXES

CHIP DONOHUE, PHD

Dean of Distance Learning and Continuing Education, Erikson Institute
Director, Technology in Early Childhood (TEC) Center, Erikson Institute
Senior Fellow and Advisor, Fred Rogers Center for Early Learning
and Children's Media at Saint Vincent College

Foreword

Every Child Needs a Media Mentor

I recently watched a video on Facebook in which well-known celebrities thanked a particular teacher who helped them along the way and influenced who they became. It got me thinking about teachers, role models, and mentors and how these important adults can impact the life of a child, never knowing just how great a difference they've made. Fred Rogers said:

> Each one of us here has people who have helped us come this far in our lives. *Nobody* gets to be a competent human being without the investment of others. (Fred Rogers, keynote address, Annual Conference of the National Association for the Education of Young Children, Anaheim, California, 1993)

Who helped you navigate your childhood? Perhaps it was a parent or sibling, a friend, or a neighbor. Maybe it was a teacher, a coach, or a librarian.

Every child needs a media mentor. Every parent or caregiver needs a media mentor. But in the fast-paced digital age, where do we find these trusted tour guides and role models? In the past few years I've been delighted to see the emergence of media mentors for children and parents in many settings, including libraries, children's museums, out-of-school-time programs, child-care programs, schools and early childhood settings, and home visiting programs.

Media mentorship is being embraced by librarians and literacy specialists, children's museum staff, early childhood educators, child life specialists, pediatric health providers, home visitors, parent educators, and others who support children and their families. I've come to understand that media mentors come in all shapes and sizes, from formal and informal learning environments, with diverse academic backgrounds and preparation, and with a wide range of attitudes and dispositions about the role of technology and digital media in the lives of children. But what does it take to become a trusted source, role model, and media mentor who can guide children, parents, caregivers, and families as they select and use media?

In this wonderful and timely book for librarians and literacy specialists, Cen Campbell (my media mentor) and Claudia Haines describe what media mentorship is and what it can look like in libraries. They offer tangible and authentic examples and case studies of what it looks like when librarians take on the role of media mentor for children, parents, and the community. They've assembled a tool kit for would-be media mentors to help support children, parents, caregivers, and families in their media use and choices.

Campbell and Haines have identified trends in digital media that have had or will have an impact on libraries and librarians, including apps, e-books, and multi–touch screens as well as coding and makerspaces that promote the child as a media creator, not just a media consumer. They have described what it means to be a digital-age librarian working at the intersection of child development, early learning, literacy development, and children's media. And they have reminded us that librarians are well prepared and uniquely suited for media mentorship, with knowledge and skills in curating and evaluating high-quality, age-appropriate media, matching media tools and content to the individual child, and modeling effective, intentional, and appropriate use of all types of media with children.

Twenty-first-century learners need twenty-first-century teachers and role models. They need media mentors who have strengthened their own digital media literacy and are curious about the when, how, where, and who of new media tools. They need media innovators who want to address access and equity issues, promote language and literacy, open new doors for communicating with families, and create new opportunities for technology-mediated professional learning through collaborating with other librarians and connecting with media mentors in informal and formal settings.

This book reminds us that media mentorship by its nature is built on a relationship. When the selection and use of digital media are also grounded in relationships, opportunities for joint engagement and enhanced learning increase. Children and their families need relationships with mindful media mentors who are positive, enthusiastic tour guides and curious co-explorers in the digital age.

> My hunch is that if we allow ourselves to give who we really are to the children in our care, we will some way inspire cartwheels in their hearts. (Fred Rogers, keynote address, Annual Conference of the National Association for the Education of Young Children, Anaheim, California, 1993)

Who inspired cartwheels in your heart as a child? Who would you like to thank for being your mentor and role model? Honor their impact on you by embracing media mentorship and becoming a media mentor who brings all of who you really are to your work with children and their parents, caregivers, and families. The authors have gathered ideas, examples, and prompts to encourage and enrich you on the way. And they have reminded us that it's not about technology, it's about the relationships.

CLAUDIA HAINES AND
CEN CAMPBELL

Preface

Long before the term *media mentorship* came to be, a group of children's librarians was talking about this new thing called the iPad and what its use would mean for families, literacy, and libraries. First as part of informal discussions, then during conference sessions, and later on LittleeLit.com and other platforms, those of us leading storytimes, hosting after-school programs, and helping caregivers access needed information were trying to figure out how to use the (then) new technology that families were bringing to the library and using at home. The group of librarians grew to include early childhood experts, educators, researchers, and parents. We all had one common goal—to meet the media, information, and literacy needs of families. Over time we unearthed research, documented examples of promising practices, and shared challenges and successes in a way that created a conversation that spanned the profession and made connections across disciplines with similar goals.

Lisa Guernsey, a friend to our group of collaborators from the beginning, recognized the role librarians could easily play in supporting families as they navigate the "digital Wild West" and in 2012 used her TED talk to introduce the idea of media mentorship. This new name for our evolving job description was immediately embraced by many youth services staff members and by the

Association for Library Service to Children (ALSC), which would later publish the white paper *Media Mentorship in Libraries Serving Youth* (see appendix
A) written by the two of us along with Amy Koester and Dorothy Stoltz. The
white paper was pivotal in broadening the conversation about librarians as
media mentors within and outside the field.

As we discussed the idea of librarians as media mentors and defined what
media mentorship meant, one question kept coming up: What does a media
mentor look like? The need for media mentorship was obvious in the daily
goings-on at any public library, in the news, and in discussions on electronic
discussion lists and social media, but *how* to be a media mentor when those
media were changing and continue to change at a rapid rate was less obvious for
many. What was the best recipe for successful media mentorship? How do we
continue to engage all families with information and literacy support? How do
we connect family members with each other while using the latest media? As
with chocolate chip cookies—whether homemade or bakery-bought, nut-full
or nut-less, with dark or milk chocolate, gluten-free, or vegan—media mentors take the fundamentals and fiddle with the ingredients, finding success in
different ways that are customized to their community's needs. Although the
white paper helped identify a common understanding of the idea of media
mentorship, *Becoming a Media Mentor,* written in collaboration with ALSC,
aims to show youth services staff what media mentorship looks like and to
empower each and every one of us to support families using the best ingredients and tools available. It's a cookbook of sorts and provides the recipes
youth services staff need to cook up their own batch of media mentorship.

Acknowledgments

We would like to thank the following people for contributing to this book:

Our fellow ALSC white paper authors Amy Koester and Dorothy Stoltz; ALSC staff, especially Laura Schulte-Cooper; and Jamie Santoro at ALA Editions for shepherding all of us.

A special "Thank You!" to Chip Donohue for being a mentor to us since the beginning.

Voices from the Field

Jason Boog

Donna Celano, PhD

Lisa Guernsey

Sarah Houghton

Carisa Kluver

Michael Levine, PhD

Professor Susan B. Neuman

Michael Robb, PhD

Media Mentors in Action

Annabelle Blackman

Carissa Christner

Kelly Czarnecki

AnnMarie Hurtado

Collette Jakubowicz

Bethany Klem

Julie Koslowsky

Elizabeth Lynch

Kathleen McPherson-Glynn

Theresa Ramos

Kelly Von Zee

Sarah Winchowky

And to Everyone Who Gave Us Their Thoughts and Time

Amanda Armstrong

Carissa Christner

Kevin Clark, PhD

Ernie Cox

Dr. Betsy Diamant-Cohen

Ann Dixon

Genesis Hansen

Maren Hunt

Amy Koester

Jack Makled

Marianne Martens, PhD

April Mazza

J. Elizabeth Mills

Tinna Mills

Jamie Campbell Naidoo, PhD

Jenna Nemec-Loise

Mary Beth Parks

Kiera Parrott

Paul Sims

K-Fai Steele

Dr. Mega Subramaniam

Sarah Vaala

Dr. Jason Yip

Introduction

How to Use This Book

Becoming a Media Mentor is divided into two parts. Part I consists of seven chapters filled with background and supportive information important for media mentors. The chapters flow from research to practice. We've gathered expert insights on the topics important to mentoring kids, teens, and families and married them with the perspectives of practitioners. Chapters include discussion on research, diversity, management, working with families, professional development, and, finally, three ways to be a media mentor. Each chapter includes Voices from the Field—contributions from researchers, librarians, educators, and experts who believe in media mentorship and the role youth services staff can play.

Part II of the book features three types of media mentorship (discussed in chapter 7) with twelve specific examples from libraries across the United States. Urban and rural libraries are included, big and small budgets are represented, and simple and more complex initiatives and projects are shared. The examples of media advisory, programming, and access to high-quality, curated media involve apps, certainly, but also many other kinds of new and traditional media, because media mentorship is not just about apps. Apps are a relatively new format that has captured the attention of libraries and librarians, but they are not the only form of new media that families are consuming. Each inspirational mentorship recipe for success details the ingredients each mentor used to support kids, teens, and families, including information about target age group, media used, staff necessary, and associated costs.

There has been a significant early childhood focus in the discussion about children and technology, stemming partially from the American Academy of Pediatrics recommendations (past and present) and from notable work of organizations like the TEC (Technology in Early Childhood) Center at Erikson Institute and the Fred Rogers Center for Early Learning and Children's Media at St. Vincent College. This book, however, goes farther. Libraries serve families from birth until death, and youth services staff play a key role in supporting children and teens ages 0 to 14. This book is written for anyone who works in a library with young people and their families—including children's librarians, library administrators and managers, and youth services staff. Nomenclature for this type of library practitioner varies from library to library, so for simplicity's sake this book mostly uses the phrase "youth services staff" to refer to anyone who serves in this capacity in a community, though other terms like "children's librarians" or "library staff" are used as well, depending on the context.

We hope this book will be a catalyst for conversation, innovation, and connection. Discussions about media mentorship and how to use research and our professional experience to support families must continue. So much of our work as youth services staff is guided by one common goal—to support the development of healthy relationships and lifelong learning among human beings. As media mentors we do just that with whatever media or technology is best.

PART I

Becoming a Media Mentor

1
What Is a Media Mentor?

*The term "media mentorship" is a new one that has emerged with
the prevalence of new, or digital, media, but the concept of supporting
families is nothing new at all to children's librarians.*

—Amy Koester

A mother and child walk into their community's small public library on
a Saturday afternoon. The young child is excited to learn more about
dinosaurs. As the duo enter the children's section of the library, they almost
stumble into a family leaving the area with stacks of . . . dinosaur books. The
mom immediately starts to worry that her future paleontologist, unaware
that many of the books she might have wanted just left the building, will have
to leave the library empty-handed. After all, how many books can the library
have on dinosaurs?

Hesitantly, the mom approaches the children's librarian. She explains their
mission and gets ready for the bad news—surely there are no dinosaur books
left. The librarian, however, explains that although a family just checked out
what the library had in the nonfiction section, there are some other options for
the young dinosaur fan. With a sigh of relief, the mom looks at her daughter,

whose grin widens. After a couple of questions, the librarian proceeds to share the other resources the library has, including *National Geographic Kids* magazines; kid-friendly, informational DVDs; a Smithsonian dinosaur app on the library's mounted iPad; links to age-appropriate and authoritative websites for kids that the two can explore on the library's computers or at home; books requested from another library that will take a few days to arrive; a dinosaur game that the two can borrow with their library card; and an upcoming visit by the dinosaur expert at the local museum. The mom takes a flyer about the program and a brochure about recommended apps for kids and heads off to explore the magazines with her daughter. An hour later they leave with a puzzle and plan to check out the suggested websites together at home.

In 2010, something happened that rapidly accelerated the evolution of the children's librarian's role—Apple launched the iPad. Before the iPad, helping families access information and supporting their literacy and media needs meant connecting them with paper books, a limited number of online resources, books on tape or CD, and movies. The iPad, and the many mobile digital devices that have followed it, has increased opportunities to support families with a variety of needs. Sometimes the library doesn't have exactly what a family needs or wants in the building, and digital content makes sense for that family. The deluge of apps, devices, and online resources, however, has brought with it additional challenges. With over eighty thousand *educational* apps for the iPad,[1] and new forms of media beyond apps emerging on the market, families struggle to identify which media are right for them, which ones are high quality, which support their child's or teen's literacy needs, and which work where and how families need them. Families need help. They need a media mentor.

YOUTH SERVICES STAFF AS MEDIA MENTORS

What *is* a media mentor? As the preceding story exemplifies, a media mentor supports the literacy, information, and media needs of children, teens, and their families. Media mentorship has long taken place in reference interviews in the form of recommendations from the library's curated collection, but the recent explosion of nonbook forms of media developed especially for children, and the widespread use of mobile digital media among young children and their families,[2] demands that library staff apply their traditional skills to new media (see the accompanying text box).

The pervasive need to help families navigate the "digital Wild West"[3] has been articulated clearly outside the library world. Lisa Guernsey, author and director of the Early Education Initiative and the Learning Technologies Project in the Education Policy Program at New America, specifically called on librarians to act as media mentors in her 2014 talk at TEDx MidAtlantic.[4]

The term *new media* refers to all media that use text, sound, images, and video in a digital setting and can include e-books, apps, digital music, Makey Makeys, websites, robots, digital audiobooks, computer programs, paper circuits, movies, and more. The emphasis is on *new*, and media mentors will need to consider the latest examples of new media for inclusion in library collections, programs, and conversations with kids, teens, and their families as the technology evolves and new formats become available.

Again, in 2015, Guernsey, this time with coauthor Michael Levine, wrote in *Tap, Click, Read* that

> [m]edia mentors . . . can lessen frustration, help children find more engaging materials, prompt teachers and childcare providers to be more selective about materials, and give parents some encouragement to see themselves as part of their children's learning. They could be valuable partners for media developers as well. . . . Wouldn't coping with the avalanche of technology be easier and less stressful if those of us raising and working with children had a guide with this kind of expertise at our side?[5]

Individual librarians and library staff across the United States and Canada answered with a resounding yes, and the Association for Library Service to Children (ALSC) commissioned and adopted a white paper entitled *Media Mentorship in Libraries Serving Youth* (2015) to help guide the youth services profession.

Key positions from *Media Mentorship in Libraries Serving Youth* (see appendix A):

1. Every library has librarians and other staff serving youth who embrace their role as media mentors for their community.
2. Media mentors support children and families in their media use and decisions.
3. Library schools provide resources and training to support future librarians and youth services practitioners in serving as media mentors.
4. Professional development for current librarians and youth services practitioners includes formal training and informal support for serving as media mentors.

SOURCE: Cen Campbell, Claudia Haines, Amy Koester, and Dorothy Stoltz, *Media Mentorship in Libraries Serving Youth* (Chicago: Association for Library Service to Children, 2015).

ALSC WHITE PAPER

The ALSC white paper was written to unify youth services staff in their definition of what it means to be a media mentor and to offer ideological guidance on how to move forward and reenvision the role of the children's librarian. As with other professional initiatives such as Every Child Ready to Read @ your library, media mentorship is based on the most recent media research and policy work by respected pioneers. Experts from the Joan Ganz Cooney Center at Sesame Workshop, the National Association for the Education of Young Children (NAEYC), the Fred Rogers Center for Early Learning and Children's Media, Common Sense Media, the American Academy of Pediatrics (AAP), and Zero to Three, as well as individuals such as Lisa Guernsey, Michael Levine, Michael Robb, Chip Donohue, and Susan B. Neuman, support the case for media mentorship in libraries. The white paper brings together the research highlights and applies them to today's library landscape, in many cases for the first time.

A media mentor

- Supports children, teens, and families in their media decisions and practices relating to media use
- Has access to and shares recommendations for and research on children's and teens' media use

The paper also recommends that library directors and managers as well as library school professors support youth services staff in their roles as media mentors. Guidance in the white paper as well as support from management and professional development providers is crucial because as Lisa Guernsey and Michael Levine, director at the Joan Ganz Cooney Center, recently stated, "Librarians will become more necessary, not less, in the digital age."[6]

Since the publication of the white paper in 2015, research, professional competencies, and key positions on new media use have already evolved, further demonstrating the need for youth services staff to stay abreast of changes to the new media landscape as it matures. The rapid changes happening within the world of new media require youth services staff not only to encourage life-long learning among families but also to be lifelong learners themselves.

Carisa Kluver

Carisa Kluver is founder of the blog *The Digital Media Diet* and Digital
-Storytime.com, a children's app review website. Kluver has been a media mentor to the field of librarianship since 2010 and has conducted
workshops and trainings with Cen Campbell around the country, supporting youth services staff to see themselves as media mentors.

Librarianship is making great strides to come into its own with new media, but
there is still a long road ahead. I see librarians in my local library working hard
to recommend titles from new media, although it's a struggle. Print is still the
format of choice by most librarians I meet, despite a large variety of mediums
available within the public library.

Children occupy so many different environments within our society that
we have to consider their media use across all spaces to achieve a healthy
balance. This is most difficult for those of us who see kids in just one space.
Ultimately parents and families are the only ones to be the overall managers of "screen time" for kids, just as they are the overseers for every child's
overall educational experience. As parents, we may "delegate" this responsibility to schools for many hours of the day, but we can never expect the
schools or other programs to monitor this new media use for our own children completely since they spend four to five times as many waking hours
with us compared to with school (8,765 hours in a year; 1,000 average school
hours; 5,000 average waking hours—assuming ten hours asleep per day; see
www.centerforpubliceducation.org/Main-Menu/Organizing-a-school/Time
-in-school-How-does-the-US-compare).

These facts about time illustrate that the only way to support families is
to empower them as the primary educators, curators, and monitors of their
children's education. It may seem extreme to say, but every waking hour is
precious for children's growth and development. This means that families
have the honor of being their child's first and best teacher and need to be
reminded of this early and often. Starting off well can mean a world of difference, so children's librarians should focus most on the early years, before
school especially. These are both high-impact years in a child's life and a time
families are open to early intervention.

In later years, elementary- and secondary-school-age kids can be reached
as well through library programs. At this point librarians should understand
that families have varying needs. Some families will need support with English
language learning (ELL) or learning disabilities as their children matriculate
into the school system. Other families will want help challenging their gifted
children or working on specific subject areas of interest. But most families will
simply need to be supported in their efforts to scaffold their children's learning for simple school proficiency.

NEW TERM, OLD ROLE

Media mentorship is a new term referring to an old role that librarians have been playing for a long time. But the term also reflects a new way of thinking. No longer are librarians the experts on a single format (books). Library staff are now the connectors—the link between families and information in whatever format they need. Those formats may be paper books, audiobooks, and apps today, but what about a year from now? What will be the best of the new media or latest technology to support early literacy, struggling readers, or aspiring engineers? Librarians and youth services staff are already experienced and qualified mentors, but the real question is, will librarians continue to be the trusted source for families' media and literacy needs, in all their forms? For media mentors, the answer is yes.

SUGGESTED RESOURCES

DigitalMediaDiet.com

Digital-Storytime.com

Diversity Programming for Digital Youth: Promoting Cultural Competence in the Children's Library by Jamie Campbell Naidoo

"*How the iPad Affects Young Children, and What We Can Do about It*" by Lisa Guernsey

Tap, Click, Read: Growing Readers in a World of Screens by Lisa Guernsey and Michael Levine

NOTES

1. "iPad in Education," Apple, www.apple.com/education/ipad/apps-books-and-more/.
2. H. K. Kabali et al., "Exposure and Use of Mobile Media Devices by Young Children," *Pediatrics* 136, no. 6 (February 2015): 1044–50, http://pediatrics.aappublications.org/content/early/2015/10/28/peds.2015-2151.
3. Lisa Guernsey et al., *Pioneering Literacy in the Digital Wild West (Campaign for Grade-Level Reading, 2012)*, 15, http://gradelevelreading.net/wp-content/uploads/2012/12/GLR_TechnologyGuide_final.pdf.
4. Lisa Guernsey, "How the iPad Affects Young Children, and What We Can Do about It," filmed 2013, TEDxMidAtlantic video, 13:14, posted April 2014, http://tedxtalks.ted.com/video/How-the-iPad-affects-young-child.
5. Lisa Guernsey and Michael Levine, *Tap, Click, Read: Growing Readers in a World of Screens* (San Francisco: Jossey-Bass, 2015), 193.
6. Henry Jenkins, "*Tap, Click, Read: An Interview with Lisa Guernsey and Michael Levine (Part Three),*" October 27, 2015, http://henryjenkins.org/2015/10/tap-click-read-an-interview-with-lisa-guernsey-and-michael-levine-part-three.html.

2
Media Mentorship

Research and Implications for Libraries

Media is very much a part of our lives. The real research agenda is to find out how to use it in healthy ways.

—Dr. Dimitri Christakis

When Carisa Kluver and Cen Campbell led their *Young Children, New Media and Libraries* trainings in California and other states (beginning in 2013), they would often start the training session with ice-breaking activities that dealt directly with concepts surrounding healthy media decisions and young children because most of the early work centered around young children, new media, and libraries. In one activity, participants were asked what they thought or knew to be the "recommended screen time" limits for different age groups. Participants were shown a chart that looked like this:

Age	Screen Time Limit
0–2	
3–5	
5–8	
8–12	
12 and up	

The trainers would then ask participants to fill in the recommendations in the column on the right. In every workshop, the answers diverged widely. For each age group, the responses would include everything from "absolutely none; even looking at the screen will damage children's eyes" to "two hours a day" or "only if it's for school." Although the initial responses varied, what followed was always similar. At each of those first trainings, and during the many led by librarians since, these initial diverse statements stimulated complex discussions about the implications for different kinds of families that youth services staff work with—military parents who can see their children only with screen time for most of the year, families who use adaptive technologies to communicate, families who live in remote areas and rely on mobile devices to access new reading material, or voracious readers who simply cannot wait for the print version of a book and snap up the title on their Kindle the minute it is available for download. After every discussion about screen time, it became clear that the answer is always "it depends." The next question was, what does the use of new media with children and teens depend on?

The trainers would then present the reigning media wisdom—the 2013 policy statement by the American Academy of Pediatrics (AAP), the 2012 joint policy statement on technology use in early childhood programs from the National Association for the Education of Young Children (NAEYC) and the Fred Rogers Center, the Joan Ganz Cooney Center's 2011 report titled *The New Coviewing: Designing for Learning through Joint Media Engagement*, and Lisa Guernsey's book *Screen Time: How Electronic Media—From Baby Videos to Educational Software—Affects Your Young Child*. These four research-based documents (the most recent available at the time) became profoundly important in the discussion with youth services staff because of concepts that each offered. The documents transformed vague, and often subjective, statements into research-based decisions.

The AAP 2013 policy statement offered insights to share with families about developing family media plans, suggested time limitations on entertainment media based on age (perpetuated by news outlets as "screen time") and recommended that caregivers monitor their children's media use in terms of time spent with media and the types of media being accessed.[1] The NAEYC/Fred Rogers statement provided a slightly different perspective. It chose to specifically define different types of digital media—interactive versus passive—and to make recommendations on use of both types for children under age 8, especially in early childhood programs.[2] The Joan Ganz Cooney Center's work on *joint media engagement*—the "spontaneous and designed experiences of people using media together"—in many cases changed the digital media experience that children and teens have (as occurs with other learning experiences) and, rather than focusing on the length of time that digital media are used, emphasized what is happening when children and teens are using digital media.[3] Lisa Guernsey's introduction of the Three C's—context, content, and the child—in *Screen Time* further deepened the discussion about using digital media with children and teens by expanding the answer to the question of how much screen time is right for kids and teens from simply "it depends" to exploring *why* it depends.[4] These four resources would later help guide *Media Mentorship in Libraries Serving Youth,* which asserts that youth services staff are well positioned to connect families with the current research about media use and to help those families make healthy media decisions.

NEW RESEARCH

Since the publication of the ALSC white paper in 2015, a number of additional resources have been published about families, children, and teens and their use of media. As with other library initiatives, it is imperative that we guide the development of our media mentor programs, collections, and services based on authoritative research and position documents. In the rapidly changing digital media environment, using research to support families as they make healthy media decisions means that youth services staff will need to be responsive, continually being aware of and sharing new digital media research as it relates to children and teens.

In May 2015, the American Academy of Pediatrics held the invitation-only *Growing Up Digital: Media Research Symposium* to bring together "leading social science, neuroscience, and media researchers, educators, pediatricians, thought leaders, and representatives from key partner organizations"[5] to discuss the role of new media in the lives of families and the effects of those media on the physical, cognitive, emotional, and social health of children and teens. The group was tasked with considering the information currently available on digital media, identifying research gaps and how best to support families through the well-informed advice of pediatricians and other health experts. The symposium considered three aspects of digital media in the lives of children and teens: Education and Early Learning, Health and Developmental Impact, and Societal Impact and Digital Citizenship.[6] Several themes and key messages came out of the discussions at the symposium:

> **Media is just another environment.** Children do the same things they have always done, only virtually. Like any environment, media can have positive and negative effects.
>
> **Parenting has not changed.** The same parenting rules apply to your children's real and virtual environments. Play with them. Set limits; kids need and expect them. Teach kindness. Be involved. Know their friends and where they are going with them.
>
> **Role modeling is critical.** Limit your own media use, and model online etiquette. Attentive parenting requires face time away from screens.

We learn from each other. Neuroscience research shows that very young children learn best via two-way communication. "Talk time" between caregiver and child remains critical for language development. Passive video presentations do not lead to language learning in infants and young toddlers. The more media engender live interactions, the more educational value they may hold (e.g., a toddler chatting by video with a parent who is traveling). Optimal educational media opportunities begin after age 2, when media may play a role in bridging the learning achievement gap.

Content matters. The quality of content is more important than the platform or time spent with media. Prioritize how your child spends his time rather than just setting a timer.

Curation helps. More than 80,000 apps are labeled as educational, but little research validates their quality. An interactive product requires more than "pushing and swiping" to teach. Look to organizations . . . that review age-appropriate apps, games, and programs.

Co-engagement counts. Family participation with media facilitates social interactions and learning. Play a video game with your kids. Your perspective influences how your children understand their media experience. For infants and toddlers, co-viewing is essential.

Playtime is important. Unstructured playtime stimulates creativity. Prioritize daily unplugged playtime, especially for the very young.

Set limits. Tech use, like all other activities, should have reasonable limits. Does your child's technology use help or hinder participation in other activities?

It's OK for your teen to be online. Online relationships are integral to adolescent development. Social media can support identity formation. Teach your teen appropriate behaviors that apply in both the real and online worlds. Ask teens to demonstrate what they are doing online to help you understand both content and context.

Create tech-free zones. Preserve family mealtime. Recharge devices overnight outside your child's bedroom. These actions encourage family time, healthier eating habits, and healthier sleep.

Kids will be kids. Kids will make mistakes using media. These can be teachable moments if handled with empathy. Certain aberrations, however, such as sexting or posting self-harm images, signal a need to assess youths for other risk-taking behaviors.[7]

A new AAP policy statement is expected to follow these recommendations in the fall of 2016.

In 2015, Common Sense Media conducted research on digital media use among tweens and teens. The researchers analyzed what media and devices tweens and teens were using, as well as how they used the media, how much they used, and how they felt about their use of media. *The Common Sense Census: Media Use by Tweens and Teens* (2015) is the first study of its kind and included 2,600 tweens and teens across the United States. The study revealed that although prolific, media use differs across age, gender, income level, and ethnicity. Researchers looked at the digital media use among tweens and teens with an eye toward improving digital media design, access to digital technology, and digital learning opportunities based on the quantified use revealed by the tweens and teens in the study and the patterns found.[8] For youth services staff, these kinds of data are useful for understanding how digital media are used and then sculpting programs, developing collections, and shaping other services based on the information.

Another important document, also published in 2015, is *Diverse Families and Media: Using Research to Inspire Design,* a guide for developers and designers to use as they create new digital media content. Based on research conducted by the Joan Ganz Cooney Center's Families and Media Project team, the guide uses "large-scale survey and smaller scale ethnographic methods to study the ways in which new technologies and media platforms are shaping the everyday routines of a diverse cross-section of families living in the U.S., especially families traditionally ignored or underserved by its media and education systems."[9] For youth services staff, these ethnographic studies and the related discussions provide further insight into digital media use by a variety of families that resemble those that visit libraries every day—those with differing family structures, home languages other than English, different household income levels, and variations in access to and opinions on use of digital media. The design guide addresses the whole family experience in the case studies' approach to digital media design, which could be helpful in shaping library offerings.

FROM "SCREEN TIME" TO "HEALTHY AND SMART MEDIA DECISIONS"

> In a world where "screen time" is becoming simply "time," our policies must evolve or become obsolete. The public needs to know that the Academy's advice is science-driven, not based merely on the precautionary principle.[10]

In research and education circles, there has been a long-standing call to reject the term *screen time* as an outdated notion. Chip Donohue, director of the Technology in Early Childhood (TEC) Center at Erikson Institute in Chicago and coauthor of *Technology and Interactive Media as Tools in Early Childhood Programs Serving Children from Birth through Age 8: A Joint Position Statement by the National Association for the Education of Young Children and the Fred Rogers Center*, states that "the key is to get away from the negative connotation of 'screen time' and from the false metric of time being the only indicator when we know now the quality of the media, the level of engagement and the opportunity for interactions with others are more significant indicators of the value of the experience."[11] Media mentors—those who connect directly with families daily—can play a pivotal role in shifting the conversation away from screen time. They can refocus the emphasis by talking to families about smart and healthy media choices in real-time situations. But what exactly *are* smart, healthy media decisions?

Carisa Kluver, a media mentor, author of the blog *The Digital Media Diet*, and the founder of Digital-Storytime.com, uses the term *media diet* as "a way to conceptualize our consumption of media."[12] In a blog post about healthy media diets, Kluver references *Wired* magazine's Media Diet Pyramid[13] from 2009, which assumes nine hours of media exposure a day for adults and provides suggestions for "optimal media health" by taking into account the fact that "quality is as important as quantity." Kluver took the idea of a digital media diet even farther and created her own Screen-Time Decision-Making Model for Families (figure 2.1), which can be used to support older children in making healthy media decisions on their own or to guide younger children in conjunction with parents or caregivers.[14]

Kluver's pyramid considers three important factors: balance, engagement, and quality. A parent or caregiver might use the model this way: For a

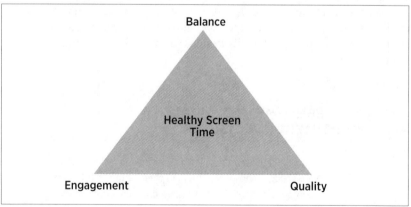

FIGURE 2.1

Screen-Time Decision-Making Model for Families

SOURCE: Carisa Kluver. Used with permission.

media request to be granted (for example, a child would like to play a game on a video game console or a mobile device), the child must work with her caregiver to decide whether all three points on the triangle have been addressed. If all three points of the triangle are addressed, the answer to the media request would be yes; if only two points are addressed, the answer is maybe, with the parent taking any other contextual factors into consideration; and if only one point is addressed, the answer is usually no. See the accompanying text box for examples of helpful questions.

The following questions can help determine whether each factor in the pyramid has been considered.

Balance

- Does this media balance other activities today (or this week)?
- Have we been on a media binge lately, or is this a break from another type of activity? Has media obsession been an issue lately, or are we expecting a lot of media use tomorrow or later today?

Note: What balance looks like for any child can change with the context—for example, whether it's a weekday or weekend, how much homework the child might have, the child's age and temperament, and so on.

Quality

- Is the media source high quality, educational, or meaningful in some way?
- Is this among the best media offerings on this topic?
- Will the child learn something important from this media?
- Can the child learn the information any other way? Is this the best way to learn?

Engagement

- Will this media enhance a relationship with a friend or family member, help bond a peer group, or otherwise build togetherness with other real people in life?
- Will it connect the child to someone far away or expand the child's social world in important ways?
- Are there any better ways to be together? Are there alternatives or ways to connect to other activities?

Voice from the Field

Michael Robb

Michael Robb is the director of research at Common Sense Media and former director of digital learning and research at the Fred Rogers Center for Early Learning and Children's Media. Michael has been involved in issues involving media and children for over fifteen years. He has published research on the impact of electronic media on young children's language development, early literacy outcomes, and problem-solving abilities in a variety of academic journals.

In a time when digital devices are so readily available, and when there is a seemingly unending supply of content, families must increasingly grapple with the role that technology and media play in their lives. There is an ever-expanding list of concerns around the amount of time that children should be using media, what kinds of content they should be exposed to, how they should behave responsibly and safely in an online world, and so on.

Parents have the same basic goal they've always had: how do you raise a good person? Knowing that children have more exposure to technology and media than ever before, the challenge is to find the good stuff, minimize the bad stuff, and be thoughtful about how technology fits into family life. For some, that may mean carefully constructed rules around time use. For others, it may be more about carving out times that are free of technology. Every family is different, so one family's strategy may not work for other families.

Librarians can play a unique, supportive role in helping parents navigate the changing digital world. As an accessible community resource, they can be a guiding resource when parents have questions and concerns. Librarians can help parents discover content that is well matched to their children's needs and interests. They can help children learn to navigate the online world responsibly. They can also provide new modes of technology-enhanced storytelling, modeling new forms of literacy practices to families.

Additionally, in the same way that librarians have long provided their own curated book lists for children, librarians can provide age-appropriate app or game lists to help parents in their decision making. Those lists can be frequently updated, and librarians can even model the use of particular media on library-provided devices. For example, a library iPad could contain folders with the five best apps for children ages 2 to 4, 5 to 7, 8 to 12, and so on, and give families ample opportunity to explore those resources.

Kluver's model, based on the years of research she has done on family media use, serves as one media mentor tool that youth services staff can give to families to help them make their own healthy media decisions. Of her own journey as a parent, Kluver states, "While I don't expect to be able to 'lead' my child in this digital age, I do hope we can go hand-in-hand, exploring this world together."[15]

It is the role of the media mentor to continually scan the research and educational environment for new findings about families and media and to help convey new information to families as it becomes available. Luckily a growing number of initiatives, individuals, and organizations, like the ones mentioned in this chapter, are tirelessly working to create a more robust body of knowledge about child, teen, and family media use.

CONNECTING RESEARCH AND FAMILIES

Youth services staff continually hone their library collections, services, and programs to respond to community needs as well as to advancements in educational or pedagogical thinking. When it comes to the use of new forms of media, it is more important than ever to be aware of the shifting landscape. Position papers, research, and educational organizations provide the requisite media mentor guidance that's necessary not only for youth services staff and families but also for libraries as institutions. With the rapid evolution of technology, research will continue to develop, and youth services staff need to be attentive and responsive in order to best serve families.

SUGGESTED RESOURCES

The Common Sense Census: Media Use by Tweens and Teens by Vicky Rideout for Common Sense Media

Growing Up Digital: Media Research Symposium by Donald Shifrin et al.

It's Complicated by Danah Boyd

The New Coviewing: Designing for Learning through Joint Media Engagement by Lori Takeuchi and Reed Stevens

Screen Sense: Setting the Record Straight—Research-Based Guidelines for Screen Use for Children Under 3 Years Old by Zero to Three

Technology and Interactive Media as Tools in Early Childhood Programs Serving Children from Birth through Age 8: A Joint Position Statement by the National Association for the Education of Young Children and the Fred Rogers Center for Early Learning and Children's Media at Saint Vincent College

NOTES

1. American Academy of Pediatrics, *Policy Statement: Children, Adolescents, and the Media,* http://pediatrics.aappublications.org/content/132/5/958.full.

2. NAEYC and Fred Rogers Center, *Technology and Interactive Media as Tools in Early Childhood Programs Serving Children from Birth through Age 8,* www.naeyc .org/files/naeyc/file/positions/PS_technology_WEB2.pdf.

3. Lori Takeuchi and Reed Stevens, *The New Coviewing: Designing for Learning through Joint Media Engagement* (New York: The Joan Ganz Cooney Center, 2011), 10, www.joanganzcooneycenter.org/wp-content/uploads/2011/12/ jgc_coviewing_desktop.pdf.

4. Lisa Guernsey, *Screen Time: How Electronic Media—From Baby Videos to Educational Software—Affects Your Young Child* (New York: Basic Books, 2012).

5. Donald A. Shifrin et al., *Growing Up Digital: Media Research Symposium* (American Academy of Pediatrics, Rosemont, IL, May 2–3, 2015), 1, https:// www.aap.org/en-us/documents/digital_media_symposium_proceedings.pdf.

6. Shifrin et al., *Growing Up Digital,* 2.

7. Ari Brown, Donald A. Shifrin, and David L. Hill, "Beyond 'Turn It Off': How to Advise Families on Media Use," *AAP News* 36 (October 2015), www.aappublications.org/content/36/10/54.

8. Vicky Rideout, *The Common Sense Census: Media Use by Tweens and Teens* (San Francisco: Common Sense Media, 2015), https://www.commonsensemedia .org/sites/default/files/uploads/research/census_researchreport.pdf.

9. A. M. Levinson et al., *Diverse Families and Media: Using Research to Inspire Design* (New York: The Joan Ganz Cooney Center at Sesame Workshop, 2015).

10. Brown, Shifrin, and Hill, "Beyond 'Turn It Off.'"

11. Chip Donohue, e-mail to author, October 29, 2015.

12. Carisa Kluver, "What Is a Digital Media Diet?" *The Digital Media Diet* (blog), http://digitalmediadict.com/what-is-a-digital-media-diet/.

13. Steven Leckart, "Balance Your Media Diet," *Wired,* July 15, 2009, www.wired .com/2009/07/by-media-diet/.

14. Carisa Kluver, "Parenting in the Digital Age: Teaching Kids to Balance Their Own Media Diet," *The Digital Media Diet* (blog), March 7, 2014, http:// digitalmediadiet.com/parenting-in-the-digital-age-teaching-kids-to-balance -their-own-media-diet/.

15. Kluver, "Parenting in the Digital Age."

3

Media Mentorship and the Three C's

Content, Context, and the Child

> [P]arents will be best served by focusing on "the three C's":
> content, context, and the individual child.
>
> —Lisa Guernsey

Although the term *screen time* (time spent using a digital device like a tablet, smartphone, or computer) may be obsolete now that we live "in a world where 'screen time' is becoming simply 'time,'"[1] it's still the title of Lisa Guernsey's landmark 2012 book, *Screen Time: How Electronic Media—From Baby Videos to Educational Software—Affects Your Young Child*, which was originally published in 2007 as *Into the Minds of Babes: How Screen Time Affects Children from Birth to Age Five*. Guernsey's book dove into the research and hype surrounding digital media use with young children and translated the information for parents, many of whom were confused by what was "good" and what was "bad." Although *Screen Time* itself is geared toward parents, it quickly became a must-read for early childhood educators, librarians, and anyone who worked with young children.

In *Screen Time* Guernsey introduces her Three C's model (content, context, and the child),[2] which can be used not only with families as a tool to help them make their own healthy media decisions but also as a guide for incorporating new forms of media into libraries. Although librarians may excel at recognizing good "content," context and individual children are often harder to serve on a community level. What are the Three C's and their implications for libraries?

MEDIA MENTORSHIP AND CONTENT

Lisa Guernsey, the American Academy of Pediatrics, and many others agree that content is often more important than many other factors, such as the amount of time spent with an iPad, when choosing the media that is right for a specific child and her family. Just as kids can get sucked into a title from the Harry Potter, Diary of a Wimpy Kid, or Janitors series and spend hours tucked away with the paper book in their lap, so can they focus for long periods on building a castle with teammates in a Minecraft Building Challenge, listening to the audiobook of *Matilda,* or reading the e-book version of *Divergent*. High-quality content, regardless of format, matters. A variety of media can make up a healthy media diet, especially if it engages kids and teens to learn and grow as readers, thinkers, and citizens. (Finding and evaluating new media, including its content, will be addressed in chapter 7, and a sample app rubric can be found in appendix C.)

Content Consumption

The Common Sense Census: Media Use by Tweens and Teens identified a wide range of young people's media use—types of media and what they do with it. The report detailed how and for how long they listen, watch, read, connect, and game. Although the study reported a wide difference in how kids and teens use media based on their race, gender, and class, it was clear from the research that young people primarily consume media rather than create it.[3] Common Sense Media's 2013 study of media use among kids ages 8 and under, *Zero to Eight: Children's Media Use in America 2013,* found similar trends among the younger set, with television watching the dominant use of digital media.[4] This trend may have to do with how kids, teens, and families have historically used more traditional forms of media, such as books, audiobooks, and magazines—by reading and listening. In this way, digital media use is more of a shift in format rather than use. Libraries continue to respond to trends in media use by offering more format options as the technology develops.

Digital media can also be a catalyst for a change in *how* kids and teens consume media. The stereotypical image of a child slumped into a couch staring passively at a large screen with drool dribbling from his lips does not have to be the reality for kids and teens using digital media. Using a tablet to drive a Sphero robotic ball, both new forms of media, through an obstacle course created by a friend or librarian requires critical thinking, technological know-how, and physical activity. A story app like *Hilda Bewildered* (Slap Happy Larry, 2015) uses intentional, well-paced digital enhancements to draw readers into the illustrated short story about a fictional princess and her fear of speaking before an audience. In both cases, the experience becomes interactive instead of passive. High-quality, age-appropriate content, especially enhanced e-books, dynamic websites, puzzle and toy apps, and many robots, have the potential to entertain as well as to compel users to make decisions and use critical thinking skills in new ways.

Content Creation: Addressing Cultural Relevancy

> Media creation provides an authentic opportunity for children to show-case and share their learning and present their narrative, especially since all children and families are not represented.[5]

Since Guernsey's book was published in 2012, the discussion around digital content has expanded to include not just content designed for consumption (reading an e-book or playing a math app) but also content creation. New media has opened up a vast array of opportunities for kids, teens, and their families to create (printable) digital books, videos, podcasts, and photos to tell their individual stories. For families who are underrepresented, or misrepresented, in published media, content creation can offer previously unheard-of learning and growing opportunities with media that reflect their cultural experience.

An app like Sago Mini Doodlecast (Sago Sago, 2013) allows kids of all ages and their families to draw and narrate a story on a tablet in an open-ended format. Users can retell and illustrate a familiar story or craft one of their own. Goodnight, Goodnight, Construction Site (Oceanhouse Media, 2014) is an English-language app based on the picture book by Sherri Duskey Rinker and Tom Lichtenheld. It allows an adult or older sibling to record narration in a home language for a child to listen to as she explores the story app. The ability to record narration is one simple way for a child to enjoy, and even share, reading in a way that supports her literacy skills and honors her cultural experience.

Chicago Public Library's YOUmedia takes content creation to another level. The initiative has embedded collaborative learning spaces in library branches throughout the city of Chicago to provide mentoring and technical resources for teens and middle schoolers. Kids and teens can write, perform, and produce music; tinker with new and old technology; design web images and T-shirts; get computer help; craft original poetry; and more. The success-ful program, started in 2009, is one of many examples of libraries offering support to kids and teens who want to tell their own stories.

Content Creation: Skills for Digital Citizens

> I believe the single skill that will, above all others, distinguish a literate person is programming literacy, the ability to make digital technology do whatever, within the possible one wants it to do—to bend digital technology to one's needs, purposes, and will, just as in the present we bend words and images.[6]

Kids and teens are growing up in an age of participatory media. Technologies are ubiquitous, and understanding how media of all kinds work has become essential. Through programming and hacking (using a digital tool for other than its intended use or in an unintended way) activities, kids and teens can develop the skills needed to fully participate in twenty-first-century conver-sations. Just as a bookmaking class helps kids appreciate how a paper book works and a "Take Apart" program allows kids to see what is inside a radio, calculator, or flashlight, programming and other digital literacy activities allow kids and teens to see how the digital media they use daily functions. Learning to write code, develop games or programs, and design websites not only allows kids and teens to share their story but also teaches them to think critically about the media they consume each and every day. Questions like "Who is telling the story?" and "Who decides what each character looks like?" become "How do I change the story?" and "How do I create characters that look like me?" Understanding how to use digital tools allows kids and teens to interact with the content in ways that empower them as learners and as twenty-first-century citizens. These are invaluable literacy skills that can also help prepare kids for their future workplace, which will undoubtedly include some sort of digital technology, both its use and design.

MEDIA MENTORSHIP AND CONTEXT

> The way parents use, talk about, and learn from media can have a big impact on how children grow up to use, talk about, and learn from it. And different types of families may look at the emerging array of tech-nology and digital media very differently.[7]

A media mentor in rural Alaska may mentor very differently from one in Brooklyn, New York, yet both support the media and literacy needs of the families their libraries serve—and for good reason: context. Each community, and each public or school library, has different resources, different cultural influences, and, thus, different wants and needs. Some libraries, like the Muldoon Branch of the Anchorage (Alaska) Public Library, share space and collaborate on after-school activities with a local Boys and Girls Club. Other libraries, like the Oakland (California) Public Library, offer free lunches during summer reading programs. And some libraries offer after-school maker programs using creative technology, like those offered as part of Maker Jawn, a cross-generational initiative of the Free Library of Philadelphia (Pennsylvania). In each case, the library is responding to its individual community, using available resources, and thinking creatively to support families and their literacy needs.

The public library, regardless of its location (or any other characteristic), is a unique community space, both physically and ideologically. Libraries, and public libraries in particular, however, share a common mission: "All information resources that are provided directly or indirectly by the library, regardless of technology, format, or methods of delivery, should be readily, equally, and equitably accessible to all library users."[8] Because community members from all walks of life are welcomed and have access to the free opportunities and resources offered at the library, libraries continue to reach out to all kids, teens, and adults to find ways to support their information needs. Media mentors must consider the individual needs and experiences of each kid, teen, and family they serve.

Media use (books included) does not exist in a vacuum. Behind every search in the catalog, every request for recommendations, every participant in a program is a many-faceted cultural context. Every person who makes use of library resources does so with her own history, beliefs, needs, and habits—in short, context. When librarians internalize their role as media mentor to families and children, the context of each interaction with a patron, whether in person or virtually, must be a primary consideration in how librarians approach the services or suggestions they offer.

The context of each child, teen, or caregiver, not of the librarian, is the first consideration. It is sometimes easy to forget this, especially when working with children and families as an "early literacy expert" or as a community helper charged with knowing all the research about what's best for children or teens when it comes to screens. However, as Amanda Armstrong, early childhood, diversity, and technology specialist, writes, "Along with understanding the context of children and families, educators (and librarians) should know their own context to understand their perspective and 'what they are bringing' to their work. This will help them notice if they are missing any elements of diversity due to their own blind spots."[9] Appreciating personal context and bias is thus part of discerning the needs of each child, teen, and family.

MEDIA MENTORSHIP AND THE INDIVIDUAL CHILD

> Discussions about the best uses of media and technology in children's lives need to also consider the functions of different kinds of screen media, what children are expressing about themselves through their engagement with these technologies, and how adults interpret and respond to children's digital media use in particular social contexts.[10]

Librarians are fortunate to be able to work with families and children in many different types of scenarios. A family might join a storytime, need one-on-one support at the reference desk, or even bump into a librarian and receive recommendations at the grocery store. Each family and each child is different, bringing their own needs, interests, and abilities to the experiences they have with the librarian at the library. As varied as these experiences are the ways in which youth services staff support individuals' media needs. Consider these diverse and familiar examples:

A young girl with dyslexia is having trouble reading any of the books on the library's shelves, but a librarian suggests an app that modifies a PDF's text or reads it aloud, which proves helpful. The librarian also suggests another app that provides reading skill practice for readers with dyslexia and might be useful for another child with specific learning, social, or developmental needs.

A young teen spends many of his non-school hours at the library instead of at home, where conditions are less than ideal and adult supervision is limited during the day. On the library's public computers and an old tablet with a cracked screen, he plays Minecraft, listens to music on YouTube, and watches videos of ridiculous antics with friends for hours, well beyond the recommended screen time. His needs are born out of his particular family experience, which doesn't reflect that of a "typical" family, if there is such a thing. Placing limits on his library computer use most likely will not result in more time spent on sports, family dinners, or reading, as is the goal of campaigns like Screen Free Week, sponsored by the Campaign for a Commercial-Free Childhood.

A mom, who discourages digital media use at home and at the library, guides her multiple children to check out armfuls of the library's newest paper books from the stacks and read quietly in the library's beanbags.

A mother and her young child stay after storytime to use the library's Wi-Fi to Skype with grandma and grandpa. They even introduce the librarian and show off the day's storytime art project!

On his way home, an older child stops at the library to do homework with friends and to use the library's Wi-Fi to download a new audiobook on his smartphone for the rest of the walk home.

A kindergartner struggling with a parent's incarceration finds comfort in Sesame Street's Little Children, Big Challenges, a series on YouTube that her family learned about at the library. The series discusses topics like incarceration of a parent, school drop-off time, and sharing. The family can access the videos on a smartphone at home or on the go.

A dad stops in to find "good" apps for his two kids to explore during an upcoming trip with long flights and extended car travel. He mentions that he'd like some educational apps, too, because they will be missing several weeks of school for this once-in-a-lifetime trip. The librarian shows him several open-ended, sandbox-style apps as well as some puzzle apps. She also directs him to the library's website where he can find various math apps with multiple levels and an option to set up a profile for each child. The librarian also points him to the digital collection for audiobooks to enjoy while they're traveling.

Each child or teen has needs dictated by her cultural context, the library's available resources, and access (or lack thereof) to media at home or on the go. When deciding how, when, or whether to offer recommendations for media use (including books), or to implement a new media service, the individual child, first and foremost, must be considered.

How does this individualization look in a program with groups of children (at storytime, for example) or when talking to a parent without knowing the child? If each child is unique, how does a librarian know what media to share, recommend, and model? How does any librarian know whether a feltboard rhyme, large-format book, or puppet is an effective early literacy tool for a specific storytime? How does a librarian know what beginning reader to suggest to a parent whose child is at home?

Understanding the cultural context and at least some of the individual needs and wants of the audience will help each librarian determine what media to use and offer. Creating healthy, positive media experiences is the ultimate goal whether that happens between child and caregiver at home or in storytime or among older children on library computers. Engagement during a program, lack of attendance at repeated offerings of specific kinds of programs, or a parent saying, "I'm looking for . . ." are good indicators to guide a librarian's next steps. Again, these methods aren't new to the work of the youth services staff, but the inclusion of new media introduces more formats, options, and considerations for supporting families. Part 2 of this book, "Media Mentors in Action," offers excellent examples of how media mentors integrate a variety of media into library programs and services, big and small.

Lisa Guernsey

Lisa Guernsey is deputy director of the Education Policy Program and director of the Learning Technologies Project at New America. Guernsey is the author of *Screen Time: How Electronic Media—From Baby Videos to Educational Software—Affects Your Young Child* and coauthor (with Michael Levine) of *Tap, Click, Read: Growing Readers in a World of Screens.*

As I have learned from talking to parent groups at preschools and elementary schools around the country, parents have a huge number of questions. I've learned to cut my talks short and leave at least twenty minutes for Q-and-A, and still I almost never get to everyone's questions. Questions are usually one of two types—harm questions and help questions: (1) Am I doing any harm if I _____ (fill in the blank)? and (2) What media product will help my child _____ (again, fill in the blank—learn to read, learn how to behave, etc.)?

What strikes me, and frankly worries me, about many of these questions is that the parent rarely recognizes or grasps the importance of context. Before answering any of these questions, I always have to ask questions myself, starting with the very simplest: How old is your child? And moving into the personal: What is your child's day like? Does she have opportunities for playing with friends, going outside, having meals with you? What does she like to do? What interests her? What makes her upset? What would you like to see her be able to do? And so on.

I can only point these parents to the Three C's and ask them to ask some questions of themselves around their family life and their individual child's needs. It is those many layers behind parents' seemingly easy questions that led me to realize that parents really do need media mentors. They need someone who can start to understand their family dynamics, start to get to know their kids, and help to guide them to see their media choices as being not only about particular books or products but more importantly about their family life, their child's daily experiences, and their hopes for their kids.

A smart media decision requires going deep. The more a media choice is tailored to the needs of an individual child within the context of that child's family, the better. For example, for me, there is such joy in finding a book, e-book, app, video, or game that excites my kids and matches exactly with what they want to do, want to become better at, or want to learn more about and—because I'm raising girls who love to make and listen to music—gets them to sing and dance around. A smart media decision is one that leads a child, and even better, a child and parent together, to feel engaged with the world and excited to learn and experience more of it.

I would hope that media mentorship would become embedded into community thinking and community practice. What I mean by that is this: Imagine the multiplying effect from having networks of leaders, parents, educators, librarians in a neighborhood all working toward helping children and their families make good media decisions and seeing themselves as learners. How great for kids and families that would be!

THE THREE C'S IN THE LIBRARY

Guernsey's Three C's model for guiding a child's media use is common sense backed by research, including the research on new media that has surfaced since the publication of *Screen Time* in 2012. This is what youth services staff do every day: use research and best practices to guide their work in the best possible way. Being a media mentor and supporting kids, teens, and families means understanding their needs, experiences, and resources and helping them make positive media choices that support them as lifelong learners and citizens. Sometimes the scenario is right out of a textbook and is easy to navigate. Other times it is not. The evolving role of children's librarians as media mentors draws on the valued practices of the past and applies them to the needs of the future. There is no cookie-cutter approach to media mentorship, just librarians learning about and responding to their communities' and families' media and literacy needs. As we keep in mind the content, context, and child in each reference interaction, program, or collection, we also must address the spoken, unspoken, and yet undiscovered information needs in our communities.

SUGGESTED RESOURCES

Digital Youth with Disabilities by Meryl Alper

From Digital Natives to Digital Wisdom by Marc Prensky

Screen Time: How Electronic Media—From Baby Videos to Educational Software—Affects Your Young Child by Lisa Guernsey

NOTES

1. Ari Brown, Donald A. Shifrin, and David I. Hill, "Beyond 'Turn It Off': How to Advise Families on Media Use" *AAP News* 36, (October 2015), www.aappublications.org/content/36/10/54.
2. Lisa Guernsey, *Screen Time: How Electronic Media—From Baby Videos to Educational Software—Affects Your Young Child* (New York: Basic Books, 2012), xvii.
3. Vicky Rideout, *The Common Sense Census: Media Use by Tweens and Teens* (San Francisco: Common Sense Media, 2015), www.commonsensemedia.org/sites/default/files/uploads/research/census_researchreport.pdf.
4. *Zero to Eight: Children's Media Use in America 2013 Infographic* (San Francisco: Common Sense Media, 2013), www.commonsensemedia.org/zero-to-eight-2013-infographic.
5. Amanda Armstrong, "Discussions about Diversity at ISTE2015," *Uncomfortable Conversations for Educators and Parents* (blog), http://uncomfortable conversations4educators.com/2015/07/05/discussions-about-diversity-at-iste2015/.

6. Marc Prensky, *From Digital Natives to Digital Wisdom* (Thousand Oaks, CA: Corwin, 2012), 193.
7. Lisa Guernsey and Michael Levine, *Tap, Click, Read: Growing Readers in a World of Screens* (San Francisco: Jossey-Bass, 2015), 17.
8. American Library Association, "Core Values of Librarianship," www.ala.org/advocacy/intfreedom/statementspols/corevalues.
9. Amanda Armstrong, e-mail to author, November 19, 2015.
10. Meryl Alper, *Digital Youth with Disabilities* (Cambridge: MIT Press, 2014), 38, https://mitpress.mit.edu/books/digital-youth-disabilities.

4
Media Mentorship and Diversity

---

*By following the Three C's, parents can make smarter choices about
when to introduce media to their kids. This means to take into account
the quality of the content (does the app or TV show have any documented
evidence of educational value?), be aware of the context (asking
questions with children and ensuring that they have a mixture of active
play and engaging activities beyond the screens), and tune into the needs
of the individual child. I would add a fourth C based on our research—
a smart media decision is culturally relevant—the media represent
stories and images that promote healthy identity development for our
increasingly diverse society!*

—Michael Levine

The previous chapter outlined Lisa Guernsey's Three C's to guide the development of healthy media decisions for families and to provide a model for youth services staff in defining their roles as media mentors in their libraries. Michael Levine has taken the Three C's model one step farther and added a vital component—cultural relevancy. A number of campaigns, within the library world and beyond, have called on librarians to address the lack of diversity and cultural relevancy in children's media and the products libraries offer patrons. We Need Diverse Books (http://weneeddiversebooks.org), Diversity in Apps (http://diversityinapps.com), and Jamie Campbell Naidoo's *The Importance of Diversity in Library Programs and Material Collections for Children* (see appendix B) all signal the importance much of the field has placed on acknowledging the culturally diverse needs of each library's community. Diversity is not just about race, language, sexuality, or family structure. It includes how different people interact with the library as an institution and the context in which they do so. What does diversity mean in regard to media mentorship?

YOUTH SERVICES AND DIVERSITY

Diversity in library collections and programs refers to cultural diversity. Culture includes shared characteristics that define how a person lives, thinks, and creates meaning. These characteristics include customs, traditions, rituals, food, dress, and language. . . . Ethnicity, race, family composition, ancestry, ability, sexual orientation, socioeconomic status, language fluency, citizenship status, religious preference, age, gender expression, education level, and domicile are all aspects of a person's culture. Children experience culture by way of their families' values and practices, in their daily interactions with others in school and throughout the community, and through the stories and characters they encounter in books, television programs and films, music, video and computer games, digital apps, and other forms of print and digital media.[1]

In a remote Alaskan village, Claudia Haines steps out of her four-wheel-drive car in front of a small school after a forty-five-minute drive on snow-covered, winding roads for a weekly storytime. The school is one of only two community buildings where multiple families and kids gather, the other being the Russian Orthodox church, so she's been invited to bring storytime here to the kindergarten class as part of a winter outreach program. In her car there is a feltboard, several folktale books, and a few puppets—all tools she uses in many storytimes. She has two goals in mind: to build a relationship with the kids and any families who stop in, many of whom rarely visit the library, and to model activities that teachers and families might use to help develop the young children's early literacy skills in both English and Russian (Slavonic dialect), the home language many of the children speak almost exclusively until they learn English when they begin school.

As storytime begins, an observer might notice that this one is subtly different from the one Haines hosted at the library the day before. This storytime includes no singing and clapping, both considered by many to be key components of a literacy-rich storytime. Although singing is often a mainstay of storytime, singing and clapping are not part of this community's traditions. Members of the community are considered Old Believers, families who value the traditional Russian way of life including cultural practices dating back to a split in the Russian Orthodox Church in the 1600s. Villagers' ancestors left Russia in the early 1900s in search of a new home where they could practice their traditional religious and cultural beliefs without persecution. Some found their way to Alaska.[2] Understanding the community's history and way of life, the librarian uses other strategies, like reciting song lyrics as poetry, to enrich the storytime visit.

Haines also brought along specific, traditional folktales popular with community families after consulting with the longtime kindergarten teacher and other community members. Using familiar stories, or retellings of traditional tales, provides opportunities to build on the children's background knowledge in one language to help them understand stories, and the included vocabulary, in a second language. Each week the teacher checks out some of the books the librarian shared.

Considering and appreciating the families' cultural experience were an essential element of this successful program and the long-term relationship that developed between the kids, the librarian, the school, and the community. As a result, the librarian was invited back for storytimes the following winter, and classes have since made annual trips into town to visit the public library. With a better understanding of the community's needs, and those of the three other Old Believer communities in the region, the librarian has since made the public library more welcoming and inclusive by hosting a Russian-language storytime, expanding the Russian-language children's book collection, and featuring culturally relevant, traditional Russian story apps on the mounted iPad in the children's room.

Much of what happens in storytime or in other library programs is guided by research. Singing is in fact one of the five early literacy practices included in Every Child Ready to Read @ your library, a research-based initiative used by many children's librarians to guide their practice. Yet, as in the preceding case, cultural values often define families' decisions about their children's experiences, with media and otherwise, more than research.

DIVERSITY AND MEDIA MENTORSHIP

> Passionate, culturally competent librarians are the foundation for change within the library profession. . . . [They] understand the power of both print and digital children's media to shape a child's view of the world and to build bridges of understanding.[3]

Kevin Clark, professor at George Mason University and director of the Center for Digital Media Innovation and Diversity, suggests that

> librarians can become sensitive to a family's or child's "context" by asking questions and not making assumptions. These questions can be asked individually if they are sensitive or as group questions. The more librarians know about the community's practices and customs, the better able they will be to determine which inquiries are appropriate given the contexts. Librarians should not be afraid to ask for help in understanding a particular context or situation.[4]

Within a community, there are individual families with unique experiences that should be acknowledged and appreciated by media mentors when connecting those families with literacy resources, whether those resources are

Voices from the Field

Susan B. Neuman and Donna Celano

Susan B. Neuman and Donna Celano, both educators, researchers, and authors, are well aware of the positive impact that library access to high-quality, curated media can have for children, especially those who live in poverty and lack "information capital." The authors' ongoing research, most recently detailed in their book *Giving Our Children a Fighting Chance: Poverty, Literacy and the Development of Information Capital* (2012), reflects the experiences in many libraries and supports the work of media mentors.

As our work in *Giving Our Children a Fighting Chance* revealed, public libraries are often the only resource for children living in poverty to access information technology such as computers and the Internet. This lack of access greatly affects low-income children's ability to use information efficiently, leading to a growing knowledge gap between them and their affluent peers. As a result, children living in poverty often do not have the chance to develop what we call "information capital," the ability to use information sources efficiently.

As we see it, children's librarians are crucial in helping to close the gap between low-income children and their wealthier peers. First, public libraries offer underserved children, such as those we observed in Philadelphia, greater access to technology. Although children who live in poverty often have access to technology during the school day, we find that their access is limited once they leave school. This lack of access during out-of-school time is of increasing importance in this digital age. Much like reading, children must use their after-school and holiday time to really become proficient with digital resources. For more affluent children, with home access to computers, broadband Internet, and digital devices, this is not a problem. But with limited access at home to computers and broadband Internet, low-income children must turn to the only resource they have to use technology: their local public library.

armfuls of paper books, stacks of audiobooks for a long car ride, e-books to be downloaded onto a smartphone for the bus ride home, or app-loaded tablets to use in the library.

> For young children, literacy, language, and culture are interrelated. Through literacy experiences, children see the values and beliefs of their culture presented in a positive and nurturing light. Language is also an important expression of culture. As young children acquire their home language, they are mastering the knowledge and skills that form the basis of their cultural identity.[5]

With the addition of new media, librarians have more opportunities to help the families they serve celebrate "literacy, language, and culture." If a library doesn't have any books on the shelf in Tagalog (the third most spoken

---

In addition to seeing that children in poverty lack access to information sources, both print and digital, we have observed that children living in low-income neighborhoods lack capable adults to assist them in becoming proficient users of technology. In our research at public libraries in low-income neighborhoods, for example, we found that children started using computers at a later age (around age 7) compared to children in a wealthier neighborhood library, who, with capable adults to guide them, began using computers at around age 3. As a result, we found that children in areas of poverty had a tendency to use technology more for entertainment purposes as opposed to information-gathering purposes. This difference also fuels the steadily growing knowledge gap, as we see children in wealthier areas use technology more efficiently to develop a rapidly growing knowledge base and develop expertise in certain knowledge areas.

Although more families in low-income areas are accessing the Internet by means of a smartphone, we do not see this access making up the difference. In reality, families in low-income areas are not using technology in a way that would help close the knowledge gap for their children. According to Sarah E. Vaala, 61 percent of low-income families access the Internet by means of a smartphone, but fewer own a tablet, an e-reader, or a computer, technologies that would help their children gain more information.* In addition, low-income families are less likely to download e-books or use educational applications on a smartphone, two other important ways that would improve the chances for children in poverty to use digital technology to their advantage.

We found in our research, however, that children's librarians are emerging as "media mentors" who can guide low-income families to help their children use information technology in more efficient ways.

---

* S. E. Vaala, *Aprendiendo Juntos (Learning Together): Synthesis of a Cross-Sectorial Convening on Hispanic-Latino Families and Digital Technologies* (New York: The Joan Ganz Cooney Center at Sesame Workshop, 2013).

language in the United States),[6] for example, or with information about Filipino traditions, what can the family read at bedtime that will allow the parents to actively support their child's early literacy in their home language? Are there online resources for the older sibling to use for a family heritage assignment? Are there apps that feature multiple languages or an option to record an adult or older sibling reading the story in the family's home language? Could the family create a book, paper, or digital, and tell their own story? Librarians may not have the definitive answer, but they know where and how to look for more options and possibilities. As Amanda Armstrong reminds librarians and educators, "Every family and community has resources, and informal educators (including librarians) need to try to figure them out."[7] Media mentorship means getting the best-quality resources to the families we serve, being sensitive to families' unique cultural experiences, and, above all, providing help without judgment.

DIVERSE NEEDS AND DIVERSE SOLUTIONS

Honoring the diversity of the communities we serve is a core value of librarianship,[8] and this value extends to every format, program, service, and collection. As noted in *The Importance of Diversity in Library Programs and Material Collections for Children*,[9] the term *diversity* relates not only to language, race, or socioeconomic status but also to the entire context in which a child lives. In serving communities, youth services staff must always strive for inclusion and understanding of the varied contexts from which families and their information needs arise. If a community's needs and experiences vary from the prescribed norm featured in the research, librarians should adapt and use their knowledge, experience, and creativity to develop positive experiences, keeping their families' needs in mind. This means thinking critically and respectfully about families and about how to connect them with the high-quality resources that work for them, in a way that works for them.

SUGGESTED RESOURCES

Diversity in Apps (http://diversityinapps.com)

Giving Our Children a Fighting Chance: Poverty, Literacy, and the Development of Information Capital by Susan B. Neuman and Donna C. Celano

The Importance of Diversity in Library Programs and Material Collections for Children by Jamie Campbell Naidoo

We Need Diverse Books (http://weneeddiversebooks.org)

NOTES

1. Jamie Campbell Naidoo, *The Importance of Diversity in Library Programs and Material Collections for Children* (Chicago: Association for Library Service to Children, 2014).

2. Wendi Jonassen and Ryan Loughlin, "A 17th-Century Russian Community Living in 21st-Century Alaska," *The Atlantic*, May 1, 2013, www.theatlantic .com/national/archive/2013/05/a-17th-century-russian-community-living -in-21st-century-alaska/275440/.

3. Jamie Campbell Naidoo and Sarah Park Dahlen, *Diversity Programming for Digital Youth: Promoting Cultural Competence in the Children's Library* (Santa Barbara, CA: Libraries Unlimited, 2014), 3.

4. Kevin Clark, e-mail to author, November 25, 2015.

5. Janice H. Im et al., *Cradling Literacy: Building Teachers' Skills to Nurture Early Language and Literacy Birth to Five* (Washington, DC: Zero to Three, 2007), http://main.zerotothree.org/site/PageServer?pagename=ter_key_language _importance.

6. Camille Ryan, *Language Use in the United States: 2011, American Community Survey Reports* (Washington, DC: U.S. Census Bureau, August 2013), https:// www.census.gov/prod/2013pubs/acs-22.pdf.

7. Amanda Armstrong, e-mail to author, November 19, 2015.

8. American Library Association, "Core Values of Librarianship," www.ala.org/ advocacy/intfreedom/statementspols/corevalues#diversity.

9. Naidoo, *The Importance of Diversity in Library Programs*.

5
Media Mentors

Working with Parents, Families,
and Community Needs

When a father borrows the delightful book Moo, Baa, La La La! *by
Sandra Boynton and reads it to his baby, father and son are strengthening their bond, enjoying the playful and uplifting aspect of life, and
learning vocabulary words, such as snort, snuff, and ruff, ruff, ruff. A
librarian can recommend a well-chosen app and suggest ways to use the
app to help parents create the same kind of heart-to-heart intimacy and
learning opportunity with their child.*

—Dorothy Stoltz

Although youth services staff are enthusiastically including all forms of
media mentorship into their daily interactions with families from their
communities, parents and caregivers themselves are modeling technology use
and selecting digital media every day for their children. Librarians are actually
mentoring the mentors. That being the case, what do parents and caregivers
need to be their children's best media mentors?

For Paul Sims, parent and librarian, the personal side of media use guides
his work with families at the library. When asked, "As a parent, what do you

want most from your media mentor / children's librarian?" Sims answered, "To make me a media mentor, too." Betsy Diamant-Cohen, librarian and early literacy expert, shares Sims's sentiment with a now famous phrase that she repeats before each of her Mother Goose on the Loose early literacy trainings: "The parent is the child's first and best teacher." Whether it's teaching their children the words to a nursery rhyme, how to write their name, or how to use digital media in positive ways, parents and caregivers are their children's most important teachers, mentors, and guides.

PARENTS AS MEDIA MENTORS

According to Alexandra Samuel, researcher and author, there are three types of parenting techniques when it comes to limiting or guiding children's digital media use:

> **Enablers:** Defer to their children's media expertise and allow children plenty of access to screen-based media
>
> **Limiters:** Focus on minimizing technology use
>
> **Mentors:** Actively guide their child's use of the Internet and other media[1]

Samuel believes parents should be mentors and "prepare . . . kids for the digital world, so they can be responsible digital citizens."[2] Yet according to her research, 47 percent of parents of preschoolers fall into the "limiters" category and 43 percent of parents of teens are "enablers," raising kids who become *digital exiles* and *digital orphans*, respectively. Samuel believes that the children of mentors, which she labels *digital heirs*, are less likely to run into trouble online and more likely to inherit their parents online know-how and engagement. She states, "We can't prepare our kids for the world they will inhabit as adults by dragging them back to the world we lived in as kids. It's not our job as parents to put away the phones. It's our job to take out the phones, and teach our kids how to use them."[3] The question is, what support do parents and caregivers need to be mentors?

PARENTAL PERSPECTIVES FROM THE EXPERTS

> Parents overwhelmingly want to do the right thing for their kids and the use of media poses an unusual conundrum. They often receive conflicting or unrealistic advice about how to balance their busy lives with the ubiquitous media that is in the atmosphere.[4]

Carisa Kluver, app reviewer and new media trainer who has been a champion of youth services staff as media mentors, did not become an app expert on purpose. She began reviewing apps (and would later publish her story app reviews on her well-respected and popular site DigitalStorytime.com) when her young son was diagnosed in 2010 with a learning disability and she desperately needed a media mentor to help her find tools to help him learn to speak. As a long-time library supporter, she went to her local public library to ask a children's librarian for recommendations for digital media that would support her son's learning. At her library, however, she was turned away because "apps have no ISBN and therefore have no place in the library." Kluver was undaunted and instead of being overcome by the "screen shame" she felt heaped upon her by that children's librarian, she used the resources she had at her disposal—a decade's worth of experience working with families as a social worker, a master's degree, a background in academic research, and her husband's expertise as a software developer—to help her navigate the confusing and new, but potentially helpful, world of apps for children. Kluver's personal circumstances, resources, and convictions allowed her to find the best resources for her son when there was no willing media mentor to help her, but her case is truly exceptional. Most families don't have the means or capability to become media experts themselves in order to make the best decisions for their families, leaving a gap youth services staff should fill. With a media mentor available to help empower a parent, there is no cause for negative feelings like the "screen shame" Kluver experienced.

Similar to Kluver, Lisa Guernsey wrote *Screen Time* in response to her questions about her own family's digital media use. Her personal experience drove research that involved many of the pioneers working on digital media use with children. When she was asked what kind of media mentorship support she would appreciate as a parent from youth services staff or children's librarians, she responded,

> Ideally, a media mentor in my children's library would know me and my family well enough to help me expand my horizons and point out new books and apps that my girls would like individually—*and* that our family would like to read or play together. In addition, I need media mentors to provide some models of how to ask questions when reading and how to listen to children's questions and discover what they are most curious about. And last, . . . I would love to get some one-on-one support in showing my kids how to use book-making apps or tools like iMovie to create and express themselves.[5]

Guernsey also cautions youth services staff as they enthusiastically practice their media mentorship skills: "It will be important for librarians to learn how to listen to families first. I've been guilty myself of assuming what parents need or want without asking enough questions. When it comes to 'screen time' especially, educators and librarians can sometimes sound too preachy."[6] The successful media mentor inspires, models, and nurtures curiosity and creativity, but first and foremost, she listens to and learns from each family's individual and unique needs and desires.

Sarah Vaala, a parent as well as a Vanderbilt University researcher focused on media in the lives of children and teens, was asked if becoming a parent changed her perspective as a researcher in any way. Her new role as parent has put her on the receiving end of the advice many experts direct at parents and caregivers.

> Already I am seeing how some of the advice that parents receive about children's media use is not very helpful to many families. In particular, hearing solely that you should drastically limit screen media from your children's lives is not especially useful, unless that advice also comes with suggestions for what media to choose and how to use it when you do use media with your children. I cannot believe that I ever thought I was "busy" before my daughter arrived. I have experienced a whole new level of busy, and I can see that timely and trusted advice about things like children's media content and use would be very helpful to many parents. Spending time scouring app stores and expert review sites to investigate and cross-reference each app just is not feasible for many families, unfortunately.[7]

If parents and caregivers are busy and need help with choosing digital media and knowing how to use it in a positive way, who do they ask for that advice? Vaala thinks "librarians are uniquely poised to become media mentors to families, as many families visit their community library regularly already— so this strategy would capitalize on time they are already spending with librarians. Furthermore, in my experience, librarians are highly trusted by families already and their expertise is valued without fear of ulterior motives."[8] Youth services staff, using their experience, evolving expertise, and responsive relationships with families, are well positioned to be successful media mentors and support their communities.

MENTORING THE MENTORS

The Mission Viejo Library in Southern California, under the leadership of director Genesis Hansen, has been a media mentorship trailblazer. The Mission Viejo Library has been especially cognizant of meeting the needs of its community through continual communication with parents as part of its digital storytelling pilot project, in surveys, and through events like "One Big Appy Family," which was a series of question-and-answer sessions for parents on topics including Expert Recommendations, Healthy Media Diet, Choosing Apps and eBooks, and Joint Media Engagement.

Jason Boog

Jason Boog is the author of *Born Reading: Bringing Up Bookworms in a Digital Age—From Picture Books to eBooks and Everything in Between.* Boog is a journalist, author, and parent who was admittedly "clueless" about how or what to read with his young daughter and ended up leaning on the media mentorship expertise of youth services staff at his local library.

App marketplaces are a swamp. Words like *educational* or *interactive* are batted around recklessly, and no parent (or journalist) could possibly sift through all this material alone. Librarians can play a big role as curators, pointing out the best apps and e-books as well as showing parents resources like Common Sense Media that will help them judge the quality of media brought into the home. Libraries should be a safe and easy place for parents and kids to explore new apps together.

We need librarians more than ever as thousands of apps swamp app marketplaces with subpar material. Parents are so grateful for any support in these crowded new worlds. Librarians can also model best practices for these new devices and apps, teaching parents how to build a healthy media diet. Tech companies and app designers have little interest in healthy consumption; they just want kids (and adults) to use these devices as much as possible.

When my daughter was 4 years old, she fell in love with Disney's *Frozen.* I took her to the library to look for the Snow Queen, the source material for her favorite movie. Our local librarian let Olive come behind the reference desk and help type the query into the catalog. Then the librarian took the time to walk us to different shelves, showing picture books, ballet books, and a book and CD set that we could check out. We discovered a whole range of materials, instead of just another Disney tie-in book from the movie.

Additionally, my daughter recently started playing with Minecraft, like many other kids of her generation. She mentioned Minecraft to the librarian, who actually volunteered to bring in her older son the next weekend to give my daughter some tips about how to control the fairly complicated game and do more with her creations. Honestly, he could teach my daughter more about Minecraft than I or the librarian could ever teach her. All of this happened on the library computers, which had the added benefit of showing my daughter the huge scope of what can be learned at the library. I am so grateful that our library, the Palisades Branch of the Los Angeles Public Library, encouraged this kind of digital creativity, rather than only steering my daughter toward more traditional media.

As part of its grant reporting process, the Mission Viejo Library submitted parental input that reflected the outcomes for which parents had hoped. The comments from caregivers were important for gauging effectiveness and guiding future programs and initiatives. According to Hansen,

> One of our focuses during the parent education programs and our early literacy classes was to emphasize to parents the importance of joint engagement around technology and how technology can be another tool for building relationships. We were very happy to get comments and stories from parents that demonstrated that they took this to heart. One mom, talking about Tablet Time, said, "It's a great class! We really enjoy coming. It's very helpful to preview apps before buying and to get new ideas for ways to play with my daughter." Another mom said, "All four weeks were fabulous. We loaded our iPad with lots of cool stuff and love doing it together." A dad told us, "This class was amazing. I spent quality time with my daughter learning about apps for our tablet [that] I had no idea were available."[9]

Many researchers, authors, librarians, and policy makers are parents themselves and bring their own concerns and questions about media use into their work. It is telling that media-based projects like Digital-Storytime .com, Screen Time, and LittleeLit.com were all begun by parents who initially wanted to find out what sorts of media relationships they wanted to have with their own children. Not all parents have the luxury of dedicating so much time and effort to such a high level of research, and this is where librarians can step in to share resources that support families to make their own healthy media decisions.

COMMUNITY NEEDS

How do children's librarians know what parents and caregivers in their communities need to be effective mentors for their children? As with other aspects of librarianship, being responsive and proactive are important. Each family is different, and each community is unique. In addition to understanding the latest research and being aware of national trends, media mentors need to ask, listen, and watch to support the families in their communities.

Asking parents and caregivers in conversation at the library and around the community what they need to know about digital media use is a direct yet informal way to better understand families' needs. Formal interviews, surveys, or polls in paper form, on a library's website, or on social media are also avenues for soliciting input from parents and caregivers.

Listening to the questions caregivers and kids ask during or after programs and in reference interviews can guide program planning, equipment and materials purchases, or informational handout development. Participating in conversations with adults and kids, even about seemingly unrelated topics, and listening to comments are also effective ways to discover families' needs. Often adults and children will ask additional questions of their peers or reveal doubts about digital media use in casual conversation.

Watching kids and teens use digital media on their own or with their care-givers can offer insight into the needs of families. Caregivers may not know how to use digital media effectively with their children and may not know what questions to ask. Kids may demonstrate digital media use that needs guidance when they use the library's computers, for example, or their own devices. Youth services staff can use their expertise to respond informally or in thoughtfully designed programs. Excellent examples of library staff responding to families' needs can be found in the Media Mentors in Action section of this book.

SUGGESTED RESOURCES

Born Reading: Bringing Up Bookworms in a Digital Age—From Picture Books to eBooks and Everything in Between by Jason Boog

Hanging Out, Messing Around, and Geeking Out: Kids Living and Learning with New Media by Mizuko Ito et al.

Inspired Collaboration: Ideas for Discovering and Applying Your Potential by Dorothy Stoltz, Susan M. Mitchell, Cen Campbell, Rolf Grafwallner, Kathleen Reif, and Stephanie Shauck

NOTES

1. Alexandra Samuel, "What Kind of Digital Parent Are You?" *@Alexandra Samuel* (blog), November 12, 2015, http://alexandrasamuel.com/parenting/what-kind-of-digital-parent-are-you.
2. Samuel, "What Kind of Digital Parent Are You?"
3. Samuel, "Parents: Reject Technology Shame," *The Atlantic,* November 4, 2015, http://www.theatlantic.com/technology/archive/2015/11/why-parents-shouldnt-feel-technology-shame/414163/.
4. Michael Levine, e-mail to author, November 2, 2015.
5. Lisa Guernsey, e-mail to author, November 12, 2015.
6. Ibid.
7. Sarah Vaala, e-mail to author, December 21, 2015.
8. Ibid.
9. Genesis Hansen, e-mail to author, December 10, 2015.

6
Media Mentors and Professional Development

*Media mentorship, like readers' advisory and larger reference
interactions, is ultimately about matching the patron with the
answer to their information need. For staff to build those chops
as media mentors specifically, it comes down to knowing what
the major resources of media mentorship are, and what they say.*

—Amy Koester

How does a library, or a profession for that matter, cultivate a culture of media mentorship? In order for individual youth services staff to successfully take on the role of media mentor, they need to be amply supported by their peers, managers, administration, professors, and professional organizations. This support can manifest in a number of different ways, such as access to professional development, inclusion of media mentor needs in budgetary priorities, hiring practices, advocacy, and moral support.

EDUCATING MENTORS

For many librarians, the path to successful media mentorship begins well before the first day on the job. Library schools across the country recognize, and have for years, that library staff of all kinds will use their skills to support families in a variety of ways, with new and old tools. Thanks to responsive and forward-thinking academic pioneers, the ideas that would blend and evolve into media mentorship have been popping up in coursework at library schools in varying degrees for several years.

Perhaps the first to formally integrate digital media into the fundamental way librarians support kids and teens was the late Eliza Dresang, professor, researcher, and author of *Radical Change: Books for Youth in a Digital Age,* 1999 among other publications. Dresang's Radical Change theory highlighted the connection between children's information-seeking behavior in the age of digital media and the transformation of books to reflect the digital world of the late twentieth and early twenty-first centuries. Like media mentors, Dresang recognized the symbiotic relationship between digital media and traditional media in the lives of kids and teens. Although not naive about the possible dangers that may accompany the abundance of information made available by the Internet, Dresang fundamentally believed in the importance of access to information for children and teens in all its forms. In 1999 she wrote, "[T]he danger of withholding information from youth far exceeds the danger of providing it. The onus is on us, the adults who care for and work with young people, to guide them to it, give them the background to sort through it and interpret it, and write, edit, and publish it in books that give them the opportunity to reflect upon and absorb it."[1] At the University of Washington (UW) iSchool, where Dresang last taught, her coursework included readings, assignments, and projects reflecting her Radical Change theory and her support of the diverse media and literacy needs of all kids, teens, and their families.

Many library and information science graduate programs across the country have heeded the call for a media mentorship approach to library service and begun incorporating coursework (discussions, research, and practicums) that supports new librarians to serve as media mentors. Classes like Youth Development and Information Behavior in a Digital Age at the UW iSchool cover such topics as theories of human development and then ask students to apply those theories to youth information behavior and digital media use at various developmental stages. Jason Yip's work as an educator and researcher at the UW iSchool Digital Youth Lab and the Joan Ganz Cooney Center is guiding development of courses connecting the design process with ways library staff meet the media and literacy needs of families and youth using a variety of tools, digital and otherwise.

Students enrolled in other programs get a taste of media mentorship also. Future librarians at Wayne State University's School of Library and Information Science are exposed to the ideas of media mentorship, and multimedia programming, in a course called Programming and Services for Children and Young Adults. San José State University's coursework for aspiring youth services librarians includes Early Childhood Literacy as well as Materials for Children, which incorporate presentations, readings, and discussions about digital media and children. The University of Maryland iSchool offers graduate students the option to specialize in Youth Experience (YX), recognizing that "[t]oday's children and adolescents need cultural institutions that can rapidly evolve their services, spaces, leadership, and programs. [The program aims to enable] candidates to design and implement policies, programs, and technology to support young people's learning, development, and everyday lives"[2]—in other words, to be a community's media mentor and meet the media and literacy needs of families.

Kent State University's School of Library and Information Science includes coursework with Marianne Martens, faculty member, researcher, author, and longtime advocate of media mentorship. Martens believes that, "more than ever, librarians need to be flexible and adaptable to change."[3] In two different classes she incorporates media mentorship and the notion of flexibility in regard to media in the lives of young people. Martens introduces aspiring librarians to media mentorship through courses like Materials and Services for the School Age Child as well as Youth Literature in the Digital Realm, in which she teaches about the ever-changing media formats that future librarians might use and what the experts have to say. Martens believes that "while it would be impossible to expect librarians to be expert users of every new hardware or software that emerges, librarians should instead focus on staying up-to-date with those technologies that would be most useful and relevant in their communities—as well as up-to-date on the research around their use."[4] In addition to infusing her youth librarianship courses with the ideas, opportunities, and challenges that will grow successful media mentors, Martens is proposing a Media Mentorship Institute at Kent State to train both current students and those already working in libraries.

MENTORING THE MENTORS: PROFESSIONAL DEVELOPMENT

Knowledge of media in its many forms is essential for children's staff. Encouraging exposure to new media through training, conferences, informal sharing, and discussion in the workplace creates an environment of support. Staff can build on their personal media preferences,

as well as purposefully train in less familiar media. Willingness to experiment, and support from supervisors for the time and resources to do
that, is essential.[5]

Depending on the library, the individual mentors, and available resources,
mentoring mentors once in the field will transpire differently. Professional
development for practicing media mentors may include participation in learning opportunities such as full-day, in-person trainings, shorter workshops,
state or national conferences, youth services–specific institutes, or recorded
webinars. Ongoing training for media mentors might also incorporate informal opportunities in the form of peer-to-peer mentoring, paid time to explore
and play with devices or technologies, subscriptions to review sources that
deal directly with new media (such as *Children's Technology Review),* and the
opportunity to try out media-based programs in the library. As with any new
skill, managers should understand that the human learning process is itera-
tive and that making mistakes or dealing with glitches are part of becoming
proficient. Many of the makerspaces researched for this book highlighted the
importance of letting kids and teens experiment, fumble, and problem solve
using their mistakes. Libraries, where many of these spaces are being sown,
must also cultivate a similar culture among staff, particularly those who will
act as media mentors for families, children, and teens.

Informal Personalized Learning Networks

As library school students move into the field and veteran library staff go about
their daily work, some may be unsure where to begin with certain aspects of
media mentorship, particularly with mentorship around digital media. Mentoring the mentors is an integral part of all librarianship, and many library
staff regularly support each other in staff meetings, as part of in-house trainings, or during casual conversations in the break room. Media mentorship is
no different. In fact, mentoring one another becomes even more important
when working with the rapidly changing world of digital media in which "tried
and true" equates to six months ago and not five years ago.

   With the plethora of digital tools such as electronic discussion lists, Facebook groups, Twitter chats, blog posts, and more, mentoring each other has
become much easier for library staff, even for those who may never see or
meet each other, to collaborate, learn, and share ideas. Storytime songs that
work best with a parachute, books that feature culturally diverse main characters, directions for exporting a 3-D design into Minecraft, and a list of supplies for the next Tween Cupcake Wars can all be found with a quick scan of an
e-mail inbox or in social media updates. The combination of face-to-face and
online mentorship helps library staff develop an informal personal or personalized learning network (PLN), "a tool that uses social media and technology
to collect, communicate, collaborate, and create with connected colleagues

anywhere at any time."[6] April Mazza, mentor to youth services librarians throughout the state of Massachusetts, believes that sharing what library staff do and find through opportunities like PLNs, especially when it's something new, is important. For hesitant library staff and those new to the idea of embracing media mentorship, "a big part is seeing the success of others in the field as they tackle these topics. Whether it be at conferences or journal articles or blog posts—the communication to others that this is not only doable but needed in our libraries is very powerful."[7] Sharing research, media recommendations, program descriptions, concerns, and triumphs is an important part of mentoring the mentors and of professional lifelong learning.

Formal Trainings, Conference Sessions, and Publications

In 2012, a panel of four librarians (public and school) presented "There's an App for That: Using Technology to Enhance Children's Librarianship" at the American Library Association's Annual Conference in Anaheim, California, to a packed house. The room was not just "standing room only"; there was, in fact, no room for any additional bodies whatsoever. Librarians were clamoring to hear from Amy Graves, Gretchen Caserotti, John Schumacher, and Travis Jonker how the newest technology at the time, the iPad, was being integrated into the rich learning environments of the Darien (Connecticut) Library, the Manchester (New Hampshire) City Library, Brook Forest Elementary School (Oak Brook, Illinois), and Wayland (Michigan) Union Schools. Apps—how to find them, and how best to use them with kids—were the topic of the moment. The audience was aflutter with questions and diligently wrote lists and notes to take back to their respective libraries.

Since then, many sessions, pre-conference workshops, and formal trainings have taken place across the country, including California, Montana, Alaska, Massachusetts, Arizona, Wisconsin, and Ohio, to name a few. What these trainings look like depends on local needs, but they all aim to share the latest research, tools, and practice surrounding media mentorship, including the use of digital or screen media. Trainings might be hour-long webinars on STEAM (science, technology, engineering, art, and math) or coding, intensive multisession trainings on new media in storytime, panels discussing inexpensive technology implementation, general presentations on media mentorship, or workshops on digital media and early literacy. Many of these trainings and presentations are designed not only to inform the audience but also to "train the trainer," creating mentors who can share the new knowledge. This method has proven to be effective and economical for providing peer-to-peer mentorship.

An excellent example of in-service training and the success of the "train the trainer" model is the Arizona State Library's grant-funded New Media Mentoring Program. With support from the Institute of Museum and Library

Services (IMLS), the statewide initiative was designed "to build capacity within Arizona's libraries to support new media offerings for young children and their families."[8] Participants in the program were required to "identify one person within his or her library or a nearby library to mentor. The expectation will be that after the initial training session, the mentor and mentee will meet for the mentor to share information learned."[9] One specific library program resulting from this training was "Tablet Time: Building Early Literacy Connections through New Media," developed by Maren Hunt, programming librarian at the Mesa (Arizona) Public Library. "Tablet Time" was designed "to give children positive exposure to technology; [bridge] the digital divide between low-income and higher-income children; and [address] the need to improve reading and pre-reading skills in Arizona children."[10]

LittleeLit.com, founded by Cen Campbell and later crowd-sourced by library staff, educators, and researchers across the United States and Canada, was a virtual space that linked trainers and library staff who wanted to share training experiences and tools in one place during a period when practice was developing in real time alongside the new tools, expert position statements, and research. The blog (now archived) and the collective voice it represented helped develop the concept of media mentorship through community discussions and resource sharing. The tested techniques and successful strategies used to "mentor the mentors" would eventually become a collaborative book for librarians working with young children called *Young Children, New Media, and Libraries: A Guide for Incorporating New Media into Library Collections, Services, and Programs for Families and Children Ages 0–5* (2015).

MANAGING THE MENTORS

> The more supervisors "see" what is happening with media and how it relates to families and others in the community, the more likely they will be to pass on to their staff encouragement and support for similar projects.[11]

Directors and managers balance community needs, budgets, staff expertise, and space restrictions, among other considerations. For some youth services departments or libraries as a whole, the concept of media mentorship is a natural fit. Performing the role of youth services librarian or being part of a library staff that works with children is dynamic and responsive work. For others, incorporating media mentorship may prove more challenging. Beyond sending media mentors to local and national conferences and encouraging staff to participate in online and in-library discussions, how do managers and administration grow media mentors in more subtle ways?

In *Young Children, New Media, and Libraries: A Guide for Incorporating New Media into Library Collections, Services, and Programs for Families and Children*

Ages 0–5, Genesis Hansen, director of library and cultural services for the city of Mission Viejo (California), provides an excellent overview of some of the behind-the-scenes factors managers must consider in their support of media mentors and the needs of their respective communities. Although tablets and apps have specific issues that managers must plan for, important considerations for all types of media include budgetary priorities, staffing, professional competencies, evaluation, space, and advocacy.

Budgetary Priorities

In response to shifting and evolving community needs, library administration will need to examine library budgets and consider how different priorities will impact spending. Library administrators, and their budget decisions, are key elements in supporting staff to see themselves as media mentors. Technology is always changing, and budgets will have to reflect that reality, whether the community wants more graphic novels, more audiobooks, or more app-loaded iPads for young children. Budget considerations might include the actual cost of a device, its longevity, and the cost of content for the device. Library expenses will never again include only plans to replace a certain number of paper picture books in a year, for instance. Instead, financial projections will incorporate initial purchases of new technology, new content, and content and device management systems as well as replacement costs, staffing considerations, and space design elements that accommodate use of the new technology. Comprehensive planning will need to include schedules for technology replacements, among other strategic decisions.

Decisions about technology will include many other considerations beyond just the price tag, however. Ease of use (both for staff and patrons), popularity among local families, quality of content, and accessibility for patrons with special needs are just some of the factors to take into account. Is TumbleBooks a good complement to the reading resources at the library, or are app-loaded tablets a better choice for families? Are iPads loaded with locally recorded oral histories a positive addition, or are such histories better stored on the library website or in another online space? Is shelf space tight for paper comics; are they popular with local teens? Would a digital subscription to the Marvel app on a locked-down library iPad provide better access to the comics teens want?

Mary Beth Parks of the Carnegie Library of Pittsburgh built on staff members' interest in learning more about using new media with families and media mentorship when she spearheaded a system-wide technology initiative. Staff training took place prior to and alongside device purchase, installation, and management planning to support a successful experience. The program began with

> researching, learning, and planning during the beginning of 2013. At this time, our children's staff were submitting proposals to be a part of

the pilot; we were pricing equipment and viewing ALSC webinars. We were doing as much research on the topic as possible and developing a plan to effectively integrate technology in our programs and services. We wanted staff to be comfortable using technology in their work and having the knowledge and resources to support children and families.[12]

Media mentors, depending on the library's structure, may play a bigger part in technology management than with other media formats. Moving forward, staff training and professional development will be vital for molding a responsive team of media mentors and serving families. Ultimately, in addition to using and modeling the new media, they may manage the devices or share that responsibility with a library's IT department, depending on the resources available and staff expertise. Including media mentors—those who connect kids, teens, and families with the resources in question—will bolster short- and long-term success.

Staffing

Hiring staff who embrace media mentorship will allow the library as a whole to best serve its community. Although still a budgetary consideration, media mentors are key to successfully meeting the needs of families. Media mentorship is not just about having a variety of books, DVDs, robots, and apps. The relationships that are fostered with the media mentor and inspired by the media mentor are essential. As with other profession-wide initiatives, media mentorship in the library is not about having the latest and greatest technology, it is about library staff helping families find the best tool and creating the most positive experience possible. Engaging families and their twenty-first-century kids and teens requires an innovative, creative, curious, and thoughtful mentor—a media mentor.

Professional Competencies

The authors of *Media Mentorship for Libraries Serving Youth* recognized that "[a]s the materials and services required by the families we serve change and expand, our core functions as practitioners serving youth change and expand as well."[13] Campbell, Haines, Koester, and Stoltz used the 2009 ALSC *Competencies for Librarians Serving Children in Public Libraries* as their guide, as do many managers and directors when they are planning staff needs and hiring new team members. In late 2015 as part of a regular updating process, the ALSC Education Committee included the idea of media mentorship in many of the individual competencies that continue to stress providing responsive and essential services. The 2015 core competencies assert the necessity for the following behaviors by youth services staff:

- Assess and respond on a regular and systematic basis to the needs and preferences of children, their caregivers, educators, and other adults who use the resources of the children's department, including those unserved and underserved by the library (I.6)
- Cultivate an environment for enjoyable and convenient use of library resources, specifically removing barriers to access presented by socioeconomic circumstances, culture, privilege, language, gender, ability, and other diversities (I.7)
- Create and maintain a physical and digital library environment that provides the best possible access to materials and resources for children of all cultures and abilities and their caregivers (II.1)
- Instruct and support children in the physical and digital use of library tools and resources, information gathering, and research skills, and empower children to choose materials and services on their own (II.2)
- Conduct reference and readers' advisory interviews to assist children and their caregivers with the identification and selection of materials and services, regardless of format and according to their interests and abilities (II.3)
- Identify the digital media needs of children and their caregivers through formal and informal customer-service interactions and apply strategies to support those needs (II.4)
- Integrate appropriate technology in program design and delivery (III.3)
- Establish programs and services for parents, individuals and agencies providing childcare, educators, and other professionals in the community who work with children (III.6)
- Demonstrate knowledge, management, use and appreciation of children's literature, multimodal materials, digital media, and other materials that contribute to a diverse, current, and relevant children's collection (IV.1)
- Stay informed of current trends, emerging technologies, issues, and research in librarianship, child development, education, and allied fields (VII.2)[14]

As with the 2009 revision of the competencies, these "contribute to a central concept: that it is a fundamental responsibility of youth services staff to meet the needs of children and their families with regard to both access to and support of digital media, and to prioritize the development of our own knowledge of these areas so that we might best serve our communities."[15] These competencies continue to provide managers, directors, and even youth services staff with goals and standards for professionalism and best practices for meeting the media and literacy needs of families.

Evaluation

Programs, access to tools, and interactions with kids and families will continue to look different in a library as the future unfolds. Already circulation desks have become places to check out books, get help with a Kindle, and borrow headphones. What will library staff do differently in a year? What service or process will stay the same? With each shift in the dynamic nature of the library, of media mentors, and of the services and programs they provide, managers will need to flex in their approach to evaluation and to decide what is successful, what stays, and what goes. Is a maker club deemed successful if five kids show up? The program costs more than a preschool storytime but has a smaller attendance. What if those five were all girls who, although generally underrepresented in computer science, discovered coding for the first time and became regular club attendees? If a media mentor spends thirty minutes talking to a family about a variety of dinosaur resources, including a paid app that the family must be shown how to access, should media advisory include apps that aren't free? What if a family wants help learning how to make an iMovie or a child needs help making a spreadsheet and cannot attend the weekend class? Is that part of the media mentor's job while working at the circulation or reference desk? Understanding the library's goals and how staff meet those goals may not be as quantifiable as it once was. Outcomes rather than outputs, along with more qualitative methods of evaluation, may be necessary to meet community needs.

Space

> Technology is not the enemy. It is tempting to operate as if supporting literacy is a zero-sum game in which the players are technology versus books. But it is not a simple dichotomy.[16]

Whether it is a simple change in seating or a major space renovation, managers must plan the library's space in relation to the new technologies. Ten years ago a listening station in the children's room may have required a small table, a plugged-in cassette player, a box filled with cassette tapes, and hard plastic child-sized chairs. Today, the station may be a cushioned window seat for two and include an iPad loaded with digital audiobooks and two sets of headphones. Although space renovations and updated configurations for new technology may require budgetary adjustments, sometimes all that's needed is a bit of repurposing or sharing of resources on hand.

Libraries have become not only spaces shared by diverse types of people but also spaces being used in diverse ways. For some, the library continues to be a space solely for quiet reading, of paper books in particular. For others, the library has become the place to access a multitude of tools and materials not available at home or elsewhere. And for still others, the library is a social space where learning and conversation go hand in hand. Shared spaces are both beautiful and challenging.

The clarity described in theories and guides often does not reflect the murkiness found in the actual, day-to-day library environment. For example, a group of young teens (12–14 years old) has grown up using a library's children's room. The glass-walled room includes the expected books, magazines, and more. Public computers in the room are loaded with Minecraft, and the library owns game accounts. The teens still feel comfortable there, even though they are older, because they can talk, do homework together, and play video games after school. Unfortunately, the teens are "too loud" or "too big" or "too rambunctious," according to young families who also want to use the space. Without a teen space that is also separated by glass walls, there is nowhere else for them to go and be social while working. What can library staff do to make shared use successful?

Library staff might consider another space in the library that is appealing to, and suitable for, the middle schoolers. If not, staff might be able to offer, or find a community partner to provide, teen-specific programs at times when different groups tend to use the same space in contrasting ways. Staff might also simply rearrange the space, providing a buffer that supports the variety of uses. Over time the solutions to evolving challenges will vary. It is up to media mentors, and their managers, to identify and fulfill the divergent needs and desires of the library's many users and to help the community as a whole understand, and even appreciate, the value of the library's unique nature.

Advocacy

Media mentors and the families they serve need managers and an administration that advocate for the services they provide and the resources they make available. Advocacy first involves understanding both the role of the media mentor and the needs of the community. Advocacy then takes many forms, some grandiose and others more subtle. It may be sharing stories with political figures about positive interactions between mentors and kids, teens, and families. It may come in the form of budget requests for equipment, conference attendance, or temporary staffing for mentors who are attending training. It may also mean advertising and marketing new, innovative programs, discussing media mentorship at library-wide staff meetings, or making presentations to the Library Advisory or Friends of the Library board. Some advocacy goes farther and spreads the word through regular newspaper or local magazine articles written by library staff about library services, through radio interviews, and through regular literacy or librarian features on the local nightly news. For families, the broader community, administrations, and political figures, each advocacy piece draws a much clearer picture of what youth services staff at a local library can do and offer, and it reinforces the library's relevance as a valuable, twenty-first-century space.

In October 2015, Jenna Nemec-Loise demonstrated another kind of advocacy. Someone posted a link to "Pediatricians Rethink Screen Time Policy for Children,"[17] an article in the *Wall Street Journal,* on the popular ALA Think Tank[18] Facebook page. The article discussed the American Academy of Pediatrics' 2015 key messages regarding media use and children (see chapter 2). The poster then asked followers, "Have you seen this yet? What do we think?"[19] The responses were quite surprising for a group of information professionals; instead of discussing professional implications, there were personal anecdotes and opinions. Only one participant, Nemec-Loise, an active ALSC member who has spearheaded the ALSC Everyday Advocacy campaign, responded with a professional instead of personal answer:

> As an active ALSC member, I'm thrilled that the AAP's new findings fully support the division's position as outlined in Media Mentorship in Libraries Serving Youth, a white paper adopted by the ALSC Board of Directors back in March. Why do we, as a profession that prides itself on seeking out authoritative resources and providing unbiased service, still respond to issues around media use with children with personal anecdotes? As outlined in the White Paper, the role that librarians serve is continually evolving. "In the contemporary youth services landscape, families engage in media in a variety of formats: print books, the bread and butter of our collections; audiobooks and audiovisual materials; and, most recently, digital media. As the materials and services required by the families we serve change and expand, our core functions as practitioners serving youth change and expand as well."[20]

Nemec-Loise advocated for media mentors not only as a leader in ALSC but also as a peer. Reminding library staff to support families based on research and experienced, professional practice instead of personal bias and referring posters to ALSC's white paper were powerful examples of advocating for families, media mentorship, and her peers.

SUPPORTING MEDIA MENTORS, SUPPORTING FAMILIES

If libraries want to support families, embracing media mentorship will involve more than attending a webinar or buying an iPad. The idea of media mentorship is shifting how libraries work and how families connect with the library

Sarah Houghton

Sarah Houghton is director of the San Rafael (California) Public Library and the author of LibrarianInBlack.net. Houghton has worked with state and national library advocacy organizations, including Infopeople, the California Library Association, the American Library Association, and the Library and Information Technology Association, and was named a *Library Journal* Mover and Shaker in 2009.

Many families, regardless of education level or socioeconomic status, do not have the tools or capacity to support their children's learning processes—to supplement what children learn at school with home enrichment tailored for their particular skills and interests. The quality of education varies widely from community to community and from school to school, so schools cannot and should not be relied upon as the only source of literacy education for children. Libraries are the only free, accessible option for families in any community to find resources, skills, and tools to help them help their children.

In order to support their youth services staff in serving as media mentors, supervisors and library leaders can say yes to children's librarians who want to pursue media mentorship programs. We can pass on these needs to our funders, asking for augmented support especially in disadvantaged communities. Facilitating the resources (funding, space, and staff time) to support multiple types of literacy education is essential to any successful library.

Library leaders need to advocate for more funding for staff development overall, including for children's staff. As with all tools and resources, if any library staff member is not familiar and comfortable with them, those tools and resources will necessarily not be passed along effectively to the community. Different people learn in different ways, so there is no "one size fits all" solution for staff development. Some combination of online and face-to-face training, independent study, conferences, classes, and reading will work for most people. It's important to listen to what staff are saying they need in order to learn. Listen and follow through!

When hiring new youth services staff, we ask for a long list of skills, including media familiarity, technology comfort, early literacy training and skills, graphic design and marketing comfort, and a lot more. I think that asking for broad skill sets instead of specifics (such as "You must be able to list ten early literacy apps for the iPad") will lead to a more well-rounded candidate and a more successful recruitment.

in a positive way. Access to innovative informal and formal education, institutional support, and collaboration are keys to a fruitful shift.

The evolution and adoption of digital technology have quickened in recent years, and youth services staff are well suited to evolve right along with it. Graphic novel collections, magazines, 16 mm movie showings, and use of boom boxes in storytime all demonstrate that the library continues to be a place of thoughtful media use and inclusion. Some librarians continue to push the outer edges of innovation while others adopt practices at a slower pace, but with their communities in mind, media mentors of all kinds demonstrate their continued relevance. The support of managers, administrators, library schools, professional organizations, and funders will help media mentors make great things happen.

SUGGESTED RESOURCES

Competencies for Librarians Serving Children in Public Libraries (Revised 2015) by the ALSC Education Committee

Young Children, New Media, and Libraries: A Guide for Incorporating New Media into Library Collections, Services, and Programs for Families and Children Ages 0–5 edited by Amy Koester

NOTES

1. Eliza T. Dresang, *Radical Change: Books for Youth in a Digital Age* (New York: H. W. Wilson, 1999), xvi.
2. "MLS Specializations: Youth Experience (YX)," University of Maryland College of Information Studies, http://ischool.umd.edu/mls_specializations#YX.
3. Marianne Martens, e-mail to author, February 8, 2016.
4. Ibid.
5. Ann Dixon, e-mail to author, February 3, 2016.
6. Tom Whitby, "How Do I Get a PLN?" *Edutopia* (blog), November 18, 2013, www.edutopia.org/blog/how-do-i-get-a-pln-tom-whitby.
7. April Mazza, e-mail to author, February 8, 2016.
8. Holly Henley, e-mail to author, November 26, 2015.
9. Ibid.
10. Maren Hunt, e-mail to author, November 25, 2015.
11. April Mazza, e-mail to author, February 8, 2016.
12. Mary Beth Parks, e-mail to author, November 18, 2015.
13. Cen Campbell, Claudia Haines, Amy Koester, and Dorothy Stoltz, *Media Mentorship for Libraries Serving Youth* (Chicago: Association for Library Service to Children, 2015), 1.

14. ALSC Education Committee, *Competencies for Librarians Serving Children in Public Libraries* (Chicago: Association for Library Service to Children, 2015).

15. ALSC Education Committee, *Competencies for Librarians Serving Children.*

16. Kiera Parrott, "Circulating iPads in the Children's Library," *ALSC Blog*, November 15, 2011, www.alsc.ala.org/blog/2011/11/circulating-ipads-in -the-childrens-library/.

17. Sumathi Reddy, "Pediatricians Rethink Screen Time Policy for Children," *Wall Street Journal*, October 12, 2015, www.wsj.com/articles/pediatricians-rethink -screen-time-policy-for-children-1444671636.

18. ALA Think Tank is an unofficial, public Facebook group, not associated with the American Library Association, made up of almost 17,000 members who include librarians and others associated with libraries, including youth services staff.

19. ALA Think Tank's Facebook page, www.facebook.com/groups/ALAthink TANK/search/?query=alsc%20white%20paper.

20. ALA Think Tank's Facebook page.

7
Three Ways to Be a Media Mentor

Media mentorship provides excellent opportunities for us to add depth and dimension to the comprehensive literacy guidance we've long offered youth, caregivers, and families. Why should digital/ new media literacy and usage be any different?

—Jenna Nemec-Loise

What does media mentorship look like? In each library, in each relationship between librarian, child, or family, and for each need, media mentorship may look different yet serve the same purpose—to serve the literacy and media needs of kids and their families. Being a media mentor does not necessarily always entail using the newest or flashiest forms of media and is not format-specific. Sometimes youth services staff mistakenly decide that in order to be a media mentor and provide media guidance to families one must have an iPad or teach kids to code. In reality, media mentorship is connecting the right content in the right format (the newest media included) with the person or group being served.

Although each librarian or library staff person brings her own flavor to media mentorship, there are three common types of mentorship. These include media advisory interactions between media mentors and kids, teens, or their families; programming that introduces new skills and lets families explore new media with someone more experienced; and access to curated media, which may include books, audiobooks, e-books, apps on a mounted iPad, or even robots for checkout.

Three ways to be a media mentor:

1. Media advisory in the library
2. Programming
3. Access to curated media

These three types of mentorship are common in many libraries but may not yet include new media such as apps, Makey Makeys, Sphero robotic balls, or conductive playdough, for example. The combination of the three different types of media mentorship, implemented in various ratios depending on a library's environment and resources, is an effective strategy for supporting families.

MEDIA ADVISORY

Media mentorship is about using, and sharing, our knowledge about what is developmentally appropriate for different ages and stages in children's lives, much the same way that we assist caregivers and young readers in navigating the range of books and other materials at different levels in our collections. It's about helping children find the most appropriate resource for their current need—best resource about the solar system for a project on the planets, a great biography for a historical person report, a humorous book for some leisure reading, etc. When a person of any age, but especially a child or a caregiver of a child, comes to the desk with a question, it is within our power to help him find the best material possible, in his preferred format, that is age- and developmentally appropriate.[1]

Supporting Individual Children

For youth services staff, the role of media mentor is a natural fit. Media mentorship is about being format agnostic and using the best media and latest research to support kids and families while considering the child's individual experience as a learner, available resources, and caregiver support. Ernie Cox, teacher-librarian and former ALSC board member, did just that when he helped a selective reader at Prairie Creek Intermediate School in a one-on-one interaction.

One of our fifth-grade guys was visiting the library today with his class. When I approached him to see how things were going, he said, "I hate reading." He locked eyes with me. This was a little test of Mr. Cox. My reply surprised him. "Please tell me more about how you feel."

We talked long enough for me to figure out he doesn't visualize much of his reading. Of course reading would suck if you were not picturing scenes. He kept coming at me with things like "Reading is boring," "I don't like books," and "No one can make me read."

I accepted all of his emotions and confirmed we could not force him to read. Then I asked, "Can you tell me about a book you've enjoyed? Maybe one that someone read to you. Have you ever had someone read a book to you?"

He looked at me like I was crazy. His eyes showed a new mood. *"Yes!* My teacher last year read to us all of the time." I suggested we look into some audiobooks (a new idea for him). As we were browsing the audiobooks, we came across *The Trouble with Chickens.* His eyes really came to life. "She read that one. I like it." We checked out the book. We set him up with the audio. He left in a different state of mind.

All of this was possible because a teacher invested the time to read to her class every day. Reading aloud is an investment in the future reader. Today it paid off!

A week later I followed up with the "audiobook kid." We talked for a bit about what he thought of the story. I handed him another book he had requested and asked, "So how many books have you read this year?"

"Zero."

"Wait. We just talked about this book. Did you listen to it? Did you follow along in the book to see the illustrations you like so much?"

"Yes, but that doesn't count."

"It counts! Hearing a story counts! Now how many books have you experienced this year?"

[*tentatively*] "One."

"Yes! Now to the next great book."

Teachers, librarians, administrators (schools in general), and parents—we must validate and affirm the many ways children can have literacy/literary experiences. Audiobooks count! Graphic novels count! If it works for the reader at her current level of growth, it counts! The alternative is to shut off pathways to success, enjoyment, choice, and growth.[2]

Cox's patient and resourceful media mentorship successfully made use of different media formats (audiobooks are one type of media) during a reference interview to serve the needs of one member of his community, in this case a school. Cox's interaction with the "audiobook kid" was essentially a form of the long-practiced art of reader's advisory but also one type of media mentorship.

As Cox's story reveals, reference interviews often already include an element of media mentorship, especially if library staff are asked device-specific questions. For example, if a parent or caregiver asks a librarian, "How do I access the library's e-book collection on my Kindle?" and the librarian demonstrates the process of finding and downloading the books, that interaction equates to media mentorship. Depending on the situation, the librarian might also suggest similar titles or suggest a related program planned by the library or a community organization.

Supporting Whole Families

At the Homer (Alaska) Public Library, the reference interview and media mentorship also merged. In this case the exchange supported not just the patron at the desk but also members of his family at home. As Claudia Haines relates,

> a dad approached library staff at the library's circulation desk looking for materials to help his fourth-grade daughter study for the upcoming school spelling bee. Beyond dictionaries, and a diverse collection of books his daughter was already reading, the library had nothing on the shelves to offer. The librarians persisted.
>
> As the librarians talked with dad, he revealed another factor important to his daughter's media needs. The family was bilingual, hailing from Cambodia, and each member of his family had a different level of English fluency. The father gushed with pride over his daughter's participation in the spelling bee as a bilingual student. He wanted to find whatever resources he could to support her. In particular, he thought she needed tools that had an audio component so she could hear the proper pronunciation of the official spelling bee words.
>
> The librarians expanded their search. They knew that the family had Internet and mobile devices that would allow them access to online resources and apps, making it more likely the librarians could find resources with an audio element. As they looked through a variety of websites and apps, the father also revealed another need. His wife was not a strong English speaker and would also likely use the spelling tool to practice her English. She had trouble making time for the classes provided by the local ESL program. In addition to spelling tools (online platforms and apps evaluated by the librarians), the librarians discovered English learning tools for Khmer speakers. Following up via e-mail, the librarians then shared online word lists for the spelling-bee-bound daughter, apps for the whole family, and ESL services for the mother.

Being a media mentor during a reference interview may involve finding resources for multiple members of a family or finding a new format of a beloved book for a selective reader. In both complex and simple interviews, there are basic elements that make the conversation, and interaction, a successful experience for kids and caregivers. The Reference and User Services Association (RUSA) outlines five components of a reference interview: approachability, interest, listening/inquiring, searching, and follow-up. These components easily apply to media mentorship as well.[3]

PROGRAMMING

> Access alone is insufficient for facilitating children's positive and fruitful experiences with digital media; there also needs to be a degree of both regulation and modeling of use by adult caregivers for the digital media experience to be productive.[4]

Library programs provide a special opportunity to share information, build relationships, model best practices, and allow kids, teens, and families to have hands-on experience with media with a mentor close by. Youth services staff have been successfully implementing these opportunities for as long as storytimes have existed and have become trusted sources for quality information and programming. Using new media, intentionally and contextually, can make some programs even more relevant or rewarding.

New Media in Programs

E-books, cassette players, and even movie projectors have long been used in storytime to engage children and their caregivers, but it wasn't until the introduction of the iPad in 2010 and the explosion of the app market that using new media in storytime became both more common and controversial. Even as recently as January 2016, the ALSC electronic discussion list lit up with discourse about apps and screen time for young children, with the often-heated back-and-forth focusing on whether storytime should include new media as part of the early literacy program. Yet, as Jennifer Nelson and Keith Braafladt wrote, "story times were never about teaching kids to read; rather they were developed to expose them to literacy practices in a safe setting and with a wider array of tools than most families could provide."[5] Sometimes the tool is paint, a feltboard story, lyrics in a projected slide, or a puppet . . . and sometimes it is a high-quality app.

Amy Koester, youth and family program coordinator at the Skokie (Illinois) Public Library, was an early adopter of new media in storytime and has been a leader in the media mentorship movement. As a media mentor calling on her understanding of current research and familiarity with the media, Koester has regularly shared and modeled the use of story and toy apps in storytime using an iPad and a large monitor.

Koester has also mentored during storytime in other ways. For example, if she read the book *Brown Bear, Brown Bear* by Eric Carle, she "would share some ideas for kids and families to explore animals even more: another animal-themed book, a visit to the local zoo, and using the tablet or computer to find pictures of real-life animals." She would "always try to suggest ways in which new media technology could supplement learning and be a fun activity to do together, and so give families more opportunities for great experiences that fit their lifestyle."[6] In other contexts, use of new media in programs will take diverse shapes. Media mentorship and incorporating new media will involve experimentation and even failure, as with any program.

Collaborative Programming and New Media

Library staffs at Michigan's Chippewa River District Library System and at the Homer (Alaska) Public Library decided to capitalize on the Internet's ability to connect kids in two spaces and in two time zones in real time. Working together, staff members created a Minecraft building challenge, expanding on the access to the wildly popular, block-based video game that both libraries already provided. Although kids and teens play Minecraft daily at both libraries, the librarians decided to offer a program that would bring players together, in the same room and across the United States, on a single server. The idea came about after the librarians met while working on the gaming component of the National Teen Library Lock-in (for ages 12 to 18), a collaboration that virtually connects teens gathered at separate libraries across the country on the same night each summer.[7]

Tinna Mills, Jack Makled, and Claudia Haines agreed that connecting older kids and teens through the popular building game had many benefits, and they wanted to make the connection possible for more than one night a year. For some kids and teens, however, access was an issue—playing the game costs money. Players (or libraries) either pay for an individual account and play online or buy the slimmed-down version of the game in app form; thus, many kids and teens didn't have access to the content creation game at home. The librarians felt they could help more kids get regular access to the creative game experience, encouraging kids and teens to play a high-quality game together. Showcasing the game at the library in a program also let parents and caregivers see the game in action with the added value of adult mentoring. In addition, librarians were able to showcase books and other resources that caregivers could use to learn about the game.

Bringing players together for the Minecraft building challenge developed new relationships among kids and teens, fostered mentorship between players with varying levels of expertise, developed positive online social skills, offered librarians opportunities to talk about digital citizenship topics like privacy, and encouraged play in a high-quality game that supports creativity and critical thinking—all twenty-first-century skills. Librarians were able to support these skills in an informal, fun environment and demonstrate their experience as media mentors.

System-wide Programming with New Media

Mary Beth Parks, children's services coordinator at the Carnegie Library of Pittsburgh, is part of a system-wide initiative to broaden support of literacy and learning in the lives of the community's children. Recognizing that children are growing up with a wide variety of technologies, children's services staff members at the Carnegie Library of Pittsburgh devised a plan to intentionally integrate new media into library programming. A pilot program, the planning for which began in 2013, was funded by a referendum that enabled the libraries to purchase iPads and other necessary equipment to be used for "engaging, interactive, and developmentally appropriate programs for children ages 11 and under."[8] The initiative also included the creation of a digital learning librarian position.

Staff received professional development from leaders in early childhood development and digital media at NAEYC, the Technology in Early Childhood (TEC) Center at Erikson Institute, the Fred Rogers Center, and Common Sense Media. Staff also sought out program and app suggestions from other librarians in the field, including those involved with Little eLit, to develop app evaluation criteria and early childhood and elementary program templates specific for their own libraries, creating a coordinated, thoughtful approach to mentoring. The initiative was successful and led to both the purchase of additional equipment and a philosophical shift among staff, who embraced media mentorship and continue to look for new opportunities to support families' literacy and media needs.

ACCESS TO CURATED MEDIA

> As consumers, the onus is on us to do our homework when searching for high-quality language and literacy apps for our children. They are out there. What are lacking are guideposts to direct us toward them and away from those lacking educational value.[9]

Apps are just one type of new media, but Sarah Vaala's research at the Joan Ganz Cooney Center and Vanderbilt University on digital media in the lives of kids has revealed something that transcends media type—caregivers and children need "guideposts" to help them find and select high-quality media, digital or otherwise. Librarians can help. In fact librarians have been curating and providing access to high-quality media since the beginning of libraries.

Librarians can easily apply the curation skills previously focused on traditional media to the new media being designed and adopted by families at rapid rates. Guideposts may take the form of recommended app lists or links to high-quality, subscription-based digital resources on a library's website. Each will have been evaluated and selected based on the librarian's criteria.

Sometimes supporting the media and information needs of families may mean providing access not just to recommendations but also to the actual content and the tools needed to use it. Public and school libraries consider families' unique needs and home experiences, incorporating the necessary tools to make access happen. In the library this support may mean providing basic Internet access, offering anytime use of tablets loaded with curated apps, or making new technologies available for checkout. (Multiple examples of access to curated media, and the other types of media mentorship, can be found in part 2, "Media Mentors in Action.") In each case, families can confidently explore the media that librarians evaluate and recommend.

Finding and Evaluating New Media

Families need media mentors because the breadth of content available for them and their children is overwhelming, as is the prevalence of recommendations on media use—both reputable and not.[10]

With over 80,000 "educational" apps in Apple's App Store, over 4,200,000 e-books in the Amazon Store, and countless new media devices being marketed to families and kids each year, finding and evaluating each and every one is impossible. Families rely on industry advertising, word of mouth, and now media mentors to help them sift through the plethora and find what is right for them. But how do librarians find and evaluate new media?

Fortunately for families, librarians are skilled at the art of curating children's materials. Evaluating digital media—apps, for example—requires similar considerations, including whether the media is developmentally appropriate for the intended audience, is well written (in the case of a story app), has high-quality illustrations, uses easy-to-read fonts, engages the child, and positively reflects the experiences of today's diverse families. But new media also has features that are unique. For example, a high-quality app should be glitch-free and easy to navigate.

Lisa Guernsey's Three C's certainly apply to all aspects of new media evaluation. A specific puzzle app might be perfect for one child whereas Squishy Circuits would be best for another. High-quality new media content and tools of all kinds present the opportunity to encourage joint media engagement (or coplay), to inspire content creation, and to support children with a variety of special needs not met with traditional media. Ultimately the media's value depends on the content, the context, and the child, and youth services staff should try out the media to best evaluate and recommend it. (A sample rubric for evaluating apps can be found in appendix C.)

Although many authoritative sources exist for traditional media, finding reviews and sources for new media may require more research. Authoritative sources have grown along with the app market, for example, and continue to inform library staff, educators, and families looking for support as they navigate the world of new media. These sources include *Children's Technology Review,* Digital-Storytime.com, and *School Library Journal,* among others. Sources may also include other librarians in the field who are experienced with using new media (apps, robots, Squishy Circuits, e-sewing, and more). Scouring professional electronic discussion lists, blogs, and other social media where experts and novices alike discuss new media will prove fruitful. As with all media curation, librarians must use their expertise to evaluate the source as well as the media.

Spreading the Word

Excellent and innovative examples of media mentorship abound, some elaborate and others simple, and they all have one thing in common—the librarians who put them into action share them with their communities. Connecting, and communicating, with families are an essential part of media mentorship, whether in a media advisory conversation, during a program, or through regular access to a variety of media in the library. In addition to offering families more ways to support the literacy and information needs of their children, the plethora of media forms enables librarians to broaden their mentorship from one-on-one interactions to conversations with whole communities. Carissa Christner took to the nightly news on a television station in Madison, Wisconsin, to share app recommendations, which she also features on the Madison Public Library's blog. Claudia Haines wrote a monthly column for a local newspaper in Homer, Alaska, to provide early literacy tips using paper books, activities, and digital media. AnnMarie Hurtado created posters to display in the library that share tips for families on using age-appropriate digital media with young children in positive ways. In each case, the communication provided mentorship, but it also let families know that their local children's librarian wanted to help them navigate the world of digital media in addition to the forms of media families traditionally associate with the library. These librarians, and media mentors like them, are using digital media to enhance families' engagement with their children as well as to introduce families to another aspect of children's librarianship. In doing so, these media mentors offer families another way to connect with the library.

Voice from the Field

Michael Levine

Dr. Michael H. Levine is the founding director of the Joan Ganz Cooney Center, an independent nonprofit organization based at Sesame Workshop, and coauthor of *Tap, Click, Read: Growing Readers in a World of Screens.* Levine has been a frequent advisor to the U.S. Department of Education and the Corporation for Public Broadcasting, writes for public affairs journals, and appears frequently in the media. He writes a regular column for the *Huffington Post* and regularly keynotes conferences focused on child development, learning, and digital media.

Media mentors themselves are on a journey to learn more about both what's appropriate for children of different ages and the types of activities that will advance children's potential. Just as librarians have for ages helped guide young children in the selection of great books to fulfill their passions for dinosaurs, dolls, or superheroes, today's library professional is a different kind of "curator-in-chief." There's so much available, and families need a hand in staying one step ahead of their children and their social group. Media mentors can help find both the good stuff and media that will still feel cool to their charges!

Media mentors should imagine a role in which they are a "guide on the side," not a "sage on the stage." As professionals we need to remain humble and keep a sense of humor or the media blizzard—what Lisa Guernsey and I have referred to as the "digital Wild West"—will overwhelm our sensibilities. Luckily librarians are trained to inquire about comprehension levels and evidence of quality and to understand key educational values. Librarians are key allies in making the transition from the digital Wild West to what Lisa and I call "Readialand," a place where human interactions remain most critical, but where tech-assisted strategies can personalize and support robust learning for a lifetime.

GUIDEPOSTS AND GUIDES

If the literacy and media needs of all families are a priority for libraries, librarians' role as media mentor becomes essential. Librarians are needed to curate new media and make the highest quality content and tools accessible, alongside the paper books, audiobooks, graphic novels, and CDs that still fill the shelves of children's libraries. As media mentors, librarians also need to extend their programming and advisory to apps, online resources, robots, e-books, and whatever is the latest new media. Families continue to look toward the free, welcoming, information-rich space known as the public library, and the librarians who work there, for expertise, access, and guidance. The informal learning environment of the library is an ideal place to inspire lifelong learning, foster digital citizenship, and demonstrate healthy media choices. It is up to media mentors to use their expertise and the resources their libraries offer to support families' needs.

SUGGESTED RESOURCES

Children's Technology Review

Common Sense Media

Digital-Storytime.com

Horn Book

School Library Journal

NOTES

1. Amy Koester, e-mail to author, October 31, 2015.
2. Ernie Cox, e-mail to author, November 2, 2015.
3. American Library Association, Reference and User Services Association, "Guidelines for Behavioral Performance of Reference and Information Service Providers," www.ala.org/rusa/resources/guidelines/guidelinesbehavioral.
4. Cen Campbell, Claudia Haines, Amy Koester, and Dorothy Stoltz, *Media Mentorship in Libraries Serving Youth* (Chicago: Association for Library Service to Children, 2015), 2.
5. Jennifer Nelson and Keith Braafladt, *Technology and Literacy: 21st Century Library Programming for Children and Teens* (Chicago: American Library Association, 2012), 8.
6. Amy Koester, e-mail to author, October 31, 2015.
7. National Teen Lock-in, https://sites.google.com/site/teenlibrarylockin/home.
8. Mary Beth Parks, e-mail to author, November 17, 2015.
9. Sarah Vaala, "New Stakes in the Market: A Researcher and New Parent 'Gets a Read on' the App Stores," *Ed Central* (blog), December 9, 2015, www.edcentral .org/get-a-read-on-apps/?utm_source=NCFL+Literacy+NOW &utm _campaign=f8d923264f-11_6_15&utm_medium=email&utm_term=0 _ddbeaff477-f8d923264f-67117105.
10. Amy Koester, e-mail to author, October 31, 2015.

PART II

MEDIA MENTORS IN ACTION

Media Advisory

APP FINDER

This project helps families looking for app recommendations by providing a searchable collection of curated apps on a library website, many of which are featured in related library programs.

Target audience:	Ages 0–8 and their caregivers
Participant number:	Approximately 347 users per month
Media used:	Website, blog, iPad, and various apps (plus projector for related program use)
Staff involvement:	1 librarian, 1 webmaster
Experience required:	Using an iPad, finding and reviewing apps
Costs:	Staff time, cost of an iPad for staff use, and cost of apps (typically ranging from free to $5.00 each)
Funding:	Madison (Wisconsin) Public Library
Partner organizations:	Madison Public Library only
Community size:	236,901 (Madison, Wisconsin)
Duration:	Ongoing

Along with the online catalog, event calendar, and information on how to get a library card, the Madison Public Library's website now features the App Finder, a database of apps reviewed and recommended by library staff. The searchable collection includes apps for ages 8 and under. Each app record features the app's title and its easily identifiable icon, suggested ages, the applicable operating system, links to the developers' sites and/or each relevant app store, whether it is paid, free, or free with in-app purchases (freemium), and a thoughtful review by library staff. Many of the apps are featured in the library's program called The Supper Club.

Related Program—The Supper Club. Many of the apps in the App Finder are featured at "The Supper Club," a monthly program for families (typically five each month) who bring their dinner to the library after work and enjoy a meal, picnic-style, while the librarian shares a collection of different apps. Afterward, small groups either work on a related craft or explore the featured apps further. The apps of the night are then highlighted on the blog Library Makers (www .librarymakers.blogspot.com).

Related Program—As Seen on NBC 15. The App Finder also highlights an app shared by the librarian in another program that reaches a wide audience. The librarian introduces the highlighted app, and tips for using apps with kids, on the local nightly news (NBC 15) every other week. A highlighted app box at the top of the App Finder page includes details about the app plus a link to the related news segment so families can see the app, and the librarian, in action.

Lessons Learned

The first iteration of the App Finder was quickly put together in response to community need, but it wasn't very user friendly. The librarian, webmaster, and branch manager put their heads together and designed a tool that organized the app records the way families needed to access them. Unlike Pinterest boards or separate blogs, the App Finder locates the app recommendations alongside the other library resources, making the library website a one-stop shop for families and their media needs.

Future Plans

The librarian in charge of the App Finder plans to seek out one or two other librarians within the library system who would be willing to review apps. The library also plans to increase promotion of the App Finder on social media and in-house with take-home flyers.

SOURCE: Carissa Christner, Madison (Wisconsin) Public Library

HOMEWORK HELP / AYUDA GRATIS CON LA TAREA PARA NIÑOS Y JÓVENES

Homework Help offers dual-language kids and teens an opportunity to get media advisory and help with schoolwork at the library.

Target audience:	Ages 5–17 and their families
Participant number:	40 kids
Media used:	Desktop computers, Mac and PC laptops, iPads, smartphones, various websites, scanning/e-mailing, printing, PowerPoint, and Microsoft Word
Staff involvement:	2 staff members plus college students, local teachers, and local National Honor Society teen volunteers
Experience required:	Using a variety of digital tools, Spanish fluency
Costs:	N/A
Funding:	Library's annual operating budget plus partnership contributions
Partner organizations:	Addison (Illinois) Public Library, College of DuPage, DuPage County school districts, USDA Summer Food Program
Community size:	37,297 (Addison, Illinois)
Duration:	2 hours, twice weekly during the school year

The Community Engagement department at the Addison (Illinois) Public Library sponsors a twice weekly, dual-language Homework Help after-school program to support kids and teens (grades K–12) who need help with schoolwork, many of whom have no, or limited, Internet access at home. The program includes both digital and traditional media advisory based on the kids' and teens' needs. Some participants need help creating digital documents for a writing assignment, conducting successful online research for a history project, or figuring out solutions to geometry problems. Two members of the library staff, many of whom are bilingual (English and Spanish), are on hand to help kids during each session along with volunteers from partner organizations, including college students, local teachers, and National Honor Society students from a local high school. Other library staff help out as needed. Snacks are provided.

Related Initiative—Family Media Advisory. Many of the kids who come to the library for after-school help have adults in their family who also get media advisory, and tech help specifically, from library staff throughout the day. The adults come to the library for assistance with day-to-day online activities. Families can make appointments for one-on-one help or ask for assistance any time. Many families rely on older kids to help them navigate online forms required for basic family needs (immigration, driver's license, free or reduced-price school lunch, unemployment, taxes), and the library staff's media advisory relieves some of the kids' burden. Many of the adults who get tech help at the library are Spanish speaking, and the library has increased its Spanish-speaking staff to respond to the community's needs.

Related Program—Hungry Brain. With a goal of increasing local teens' digital literacy skills, library staff created a program built on a book club model but featuring videos. The library's teen librarian finds and evaluates freely available, age-appropriate videos and then creates monthly playlists on the library's YouTube account for the teens to watch. The club features videos on thought-provoking topics like time travel or online shaming. The teens (grades 6–12) watch as many videos as they can at the library or on their own before coming to a meet-up to discuss what they watched. The librarian acts as moderator and curator, making sure the conversation is inclusive.

Lessons Learned

The library staff realized over time that the traditional structure of the library may not best serve families in the community. Departments began library-wide collaborations. They identified community needs and then determined what staff, partnerships, and resources would best serve families. Although the library receives some grant funding for equipment and other initial expenses, it relies more on local partnerships to make projects successful and sustainable over the long term.

Future Plans

The library staff would like to reach more families that are not already using the library's services, and the library is developing a hospital outreach program to introduce new families to the library.

SOURCE: Kelly Von Zee and Elizabeth Lynch, Addison (Illinois) Public Library

CURATING APPS ON PINTEREST BOARDS

Using popular social media platforms, like Pinterest, can offer a way to connect families with new media recommendations and support informal learning.

Target audience:	Ages 6 and under, ages 6 and up and their caregivers
Participant number:	Each Pinterest board has more than 160 followers
Media used:	iPad and various apps for staff use
Staff involvement:	2 librarians
Experience required:	Using an iPad, finding and reviewing apps
Costs:	Staff time, cost of an iPad for staff use, and cost of apps (typically ranging from free to $5.00 each)
Funding:	Pasadena (California) Public Library
Partner organizations:	Pasadena Public Library only
Community size:	160,000 (Pasadena, California)
Duration:	Ongoing

Libraries looking to curate and share high-quality apps and other digital media for families in their community sometimes look beyond the traditional online tools like their library's website. Social media tools like Pinterest are popular with library patrons, and, by using them, libraries like the Pasadena Public Library (PPL) meet patrons where they already spend time online. Using Pinterest has an additional perk—the library is using an existing tool for a community need instead of having to create something from scratch.

Pinterest is easy to use, and librarians at PPL, among others, like how it works. It lets library staff "pin" or bookmark images, like app icons, or videos to collections called "boards." Pinners can add text along with the visual piece. Sometimes the text is an informal note, but in PPL's case the pin includes the app's name, cost, a brief description, and the operating system (iOS, for example).

In addition to boards with titles like Book Love, Staff Picks, and One City, One Story, the Pasadena Public Library's Pinterest account includes three boards related to kids and digital media. One board features apps recommended for ages 6 and under, another highlights apps for ages 6 and up, and the third board collects links to information about using digital media with children from organizations like the Fred Rogers Center, UCLA, the Joan Ganz Cooney Center, Common Sense Media, and the American Academy of Pediatrics.

Lessons Learned

Families often ask about the price of the apps recommended on the Pinterest boards. The librarians added prices but then struggled to keep up with fluctuating prices and making sure the pins reflected what was current. They are considering leaving price out of the app description altogether. In the meantime, they have posted an addendum noting that prices are subject to change.

Future Plans

One of the librarians involved with the Pinterest boards is regularly invited to talk about apps and digital media at local elementary schools. For one such event, a pajama party for families in honor of Dr. Seuss Day, the librarian will share apps like Green Eggs and Ham—Read & Learn—Dr. Seuss (Oceanhouse Media) as part of an e-storytime.

SOURCE: AnnMarie Hurtado, Pasadena (California) Public Library

"TIPS FOR RAISING A READER" NEWSPAPER COLUMN

A monthly column in a local newspaper shares literacy and media advisory tips outside the library.

Target audience:	Ages 6 and under and their families
Participant number:	N/A
Media used:	Picture books, iPad, story and toy apps for ages 6 and under
Staff involvement:	1 librarian
Experience required:	Using an iPad, finding and reviewing apps, applying early literacy research to a variety of media
Costs:	Staff time, iPad, apps and books reviewed and recommended
Funding:	Homer (Alaska) Public Library
Partner organizations:	Homer Public Library and the *Homer Tribune*
Community size:	5,300 (City of Homer, Alaska) plus 7,000 (surrounding service area)
Duration:	Monthly

Following an opinion piece the librarian wrote for the local paper about the importance of summer reading, newspaper staff and the librarian decided to start a monthly column called "Tips for Raising a Reader." Each month, the librarian shares early literacy information based on Every Child Ready to Read @ your library, tips for using digital media with children, and both a book and an app recommendation. The article is both an information and advocacy tool. It is another way to support families as they grow readers and reaches members of the community who may not come to storytime or use the library. For many families, the column's content provides a starting point for conversations about early literacy practices and digital media.

The *Homer Tribune* was chosen for the "Tips for Raising a Reader" column because of a developing partnership between the library and the paper, not necessarily because of circulation size. ("Tips for Raising a Reader" runs in a paper that prints anywhere from 2,500 to 3,000 copies each week that are sold throughout the library's large service area and in the online edition, which reaches 300–900 users each week.) The library wanted to try a new approach to sharing early literacy information, so this was in a sense a pilot, and numbers were less of a factor than might be the case for other libraries doing something similar. The newspaper staff has been easy to work with, and both partners are happy with the ongoing collaboration.

Lessons Learned

Multiple factors are important to consider when starting these types of projects. Establishing goals for the partnership helped clarify decisions about how often the column would run, what would be included, and with which paper the library would partner. Sometimes relationships and circumstances prove more important than relying solely on statistics, for example. Things to consider:

- Different newspapers, or magazines, may or may not have space or the resources to manage guest columns.
- The librarian was not compensated for the articles because she was writing as a library employee.
- Articles written on staff time may need to be approved by library administration before publication.
- Writing for a newspaper is different than writing grants or for other purposes, so there may be a learning curve.

Future Plans

The success of the monthly column has inspired library staff to look for other innovative ways to reach out to families in the community. The librarian plans to develop more "out of the box" outreach opportunities as time allows.

In the immediate future the library will be switching to an open source digital summer reading platform, called the Great Reading Adventure, to more easily include kids and teens living in the remote communities of the service area, some of which are only accessible by plane or boat. The digital platform, created by the Maricopa County (Arizona) Library District, offers a new way to engage kids whether they can access the physical library regularly or not. It also offers opportunities to share literacy information and offer media advisory to registered families.

SOURCE: Claudia Haines, Homer (Alaska) Public Library

New Media in Programs

DIGITAL STORYTIME

Using digital tools in a popular preschool storytime program offers opportunities to talk about joint media engagement, finding and evaluating quality apps, and healthy media diets for young children and their families.

Target audience:	Ages 2–5 and 3–6 and their families
Participant number:	30–35 people at each storytime
Media used:	1 iPad and various early literacy apps for staff use, projector, VGA cable and speakers for projection, 7 iPads for patron checkout and use during program
Staff involvement:	2 librarians (each hosts two of the storytimes)
Experience required:	Using an iPad, finding and reviewing apps, developing and presenting storytimes
Costs:	Staff time, cost of an iPad for staff use and iPads for checkout, and cost of apps (typically ranging from free to $5.00 each)
Funding:	Bozeman (Montana) Public Library
Partner organizations:	Bozeman Public Library only
Community size:	95,000 (City of Bozeman, Montana, and surrounding Gallatin County)
Duration:	Each storytime lasts about 40 minutes. The library offers the digital storytimes 4 times in a week, 4 times per year

Bozeman Public Library's digital storytime applies many of the same early literacy techniques found in the library's preschool and toddler storytimes to new media, in particular iPads and apps. Four times a year, librarians move the week's four preschool and toddler storytimes to the library's meeting space, which features a projector and large screen perfect for sharing e-books, story apps, and toy apps with a group.

In addition to reading stories, singing songs, and playing with rhymes using the iPad and apps, librarians model how to read and explore them with young children. Tips include information on the importance of interactivity and joint media engagement as well as real-world activities related to the digital ones shared in storytime. Handouts with information about using digital media to support children's early literacy and healthy media diets are given to families during the program. Time at the end offers families the chance to try out the apps featured on library iPads and ask questions. The library has seven iPads available for checkout so families who are interested can explore the apps at home even if they do not have their own device.

Information about the Digital Storytime program and media mentorship was presented at the Montana State Library Association's Annual Conference to a standing-room-only audience.

Lessons Learned

Library staff have been very happy with the success of the program. The format works well and has sparked conversations between families and librarians about digital media. After each program, families regularly want to check out the library's iPads loaded with the same apps used in storytime.

Program attendance has been consistent during the four weeks a year that Digital Storytime replaces the regular program. The same families who participate in weekly programs enjoy the seasonal shift, knowing that the librarians will provide a quality program, regardless of the format.

Future Plans

The library is developing a media mentor corner, a physical space with information about using digital media with kids, including the handouts made for the Digital Storytime program. The physical space will complement the information for families that is posted regularly on the library's Facebook page.

SOURCE: Kathleen McPherson-Glynn, Bozeman (Montana) Public Library

GRAPHIC NOVEL CLUB

Digital tools, along with traditional media and activities, are used to engage kids in an after-school club focused on graphic novels, comics, and manga.

Target audience:	Ages 8–12
Participant number:	2–8 kids
Media used:	iPad and Comic Book! app
Staff involvement:	1 librarian
Experience required:	Using an iPad (specifically, taking photos with the iPad); evaluating apps
Costs:	$2.99 for app plus cost of iPad (already owned by the library)
Funding:	Oakland (California) Public Library (iPad) and Friends of the Oakland Public Library (iTunes gift card)
Partner organizations:	Oakland Public Library only
Community size:	425,869 (City of Oakland, California)
Duration:	1–1.5 hours, monthly

As part of a monthly, after-school Graphic Novel Club, kids used an iPad and the app Comic Book! to create digital comic strips. In addition to starring in the strips, the kids wrote original story narratives using text and images. The digital comics were then printed out for kids to take home. Creating content helped the children better understand the inner workings of the comics and graphic novels they were reading as well as work on their writing skills. With only one iPad available, the small group of budding authors worked collaboratively to create the new comics and have fun. Using the app was one story crafting activity, among several options, the librarian used to enhance the program, which also included informal discussions and booktalks featuring the library's new graphic novels and comics.

Lessons Learned

Having only one iPad, without a strong case, meant the librarian was the primary photographer and the kids had limited hands-on experience taking the photos used in the comic strips. The kids did, however, star in the photos and ultimately focused more on the storytelling portion of the activity. A small group size made using one iPad manageable and the overall program successful for the individual children.

Future Plans

Library staff would like to buy a tripod and adapter mount to make the iPad more stable when taking photos and filming video, thus making the device more versatile and kid-friendly.

The success of the program and use of digital media alongside traditional media have excited librarians department-wide about the multimedia approach to program design. Staff are also beginning to use the iPad behind the scenes to record library staff performing storytime songs and rhymes for staff and volunteer training.

SOURCE: Annabelle Blackman, Oakland (California) Public Library

HOUR OF CODE: BASIC VIDEO GAME DESIGN

This program introduces children to the basics of coding and game design using freely available, high-quality tools and tutorials.

Target audience:	Ages 9–13
Participant number:	8 kids
Media used:	Shared laptops and mice, iPads, Makey Makeys, large monitor, headphones with splitters, Internet access, Code.org tutorials (Star Wars and Minecraft), PBS Kids ScratchJr app (related program)
Staff involvement:	1 librarian, 1 teen mentor-in-training, 1 webmaster
Experience required:	Some coding experience (using Blockly or JavaScript), familiarity with the Scratch platform and the Code.org basic tutorials, a basic understanding of electrical currents
Costs:	Staff time and $30 for food. All equipment, books, and apps were already owned by the library.
Funding:	2015 Curiosity Creates grant (ALSC) and Online with Libraries grant (Alaska State Library)
Partner organizations:	Homer (Alaska) Public Library, Code.org, and Homer High School
Community size:	5,300 (City of Homer, Alaska) plus 7,000 (surrounding service area)
Duration:	2 hours

The Hour of Code was a multifaceted initiative designed to introduce kids to coding, help families identify high-quality digital media, and offer kids opportunities to use digital devices they may not have access to elsewhere. The "Basic Video Game Design" program, part of a weekly maker club, was the highlight of the weeklong initiative. During the two-hour, informal workshop, kids and teens used freely available tools and tutorials created by Code .org, Google's Made w/Code, and Scratch, a project of the MIT Media Lab. The aspiring game designers used one of the game-based Hour of Code tutorials to learn the basics of coding and then moved on to the open-ended Scratch platform to create a game of their own. At the end of the lab-style program, families and other participants took turns trying the newly created games, some of which used Makey Makeys—"invention kits" that turn everyday objects that are conductive (bananas or forks, for example) into touch pads for computers—as game controllers instead of the laptop's keyboard.

The library's website had a dedicated web page featuring information about the Hour of Code as well as links to the free tutorials used in the program and a collection of curated websites with computer programming and coding resources for kids, teens, and adults. The web page gave families easy access to all of the tutorials used in the program so kids could keep exploring and learning, and it provided online resources for anyone in the local community who wanted to try coding. A list of recommended titles ready for checkout was linked on the library's Hour of Code web page. Books from the list were displayed in the children's library and teen space.

Related Program—Coding for Young Children. Young children were introduced to coding, and to the idea of creating digital content, using the mounted iPad in the children's library. Each week the iPad is loaded with one new, high-quality app for young kids and has become a go-to source for families looking for app recommendations. During Computer Science Week, kids created digital stories with code using the PBS Kids ScratchJr app and its familiar characters from popular PBS Kids television shows.

The Hour of Code initiative was designed to economically use and draw attention to the library's diverse resources, recommend high-quality content, and engage kids in coding, a twenty-first-century skill. The "Basic Video Game Design" program would have been successful on its own, but bringing together the added elements broadened the community's involvement in the library's Hour of Code.

Lessons Learned

The program's informal, lab-style design supported multiple learning styles and interests. Some participants created digital art with code, others learned to code with Minecraft or Star Wars characters, and everyone at least attempted making an original digital game on their own without any templates.

Pair programming was originally intended to efficiently use the limited number of devices that the library owns, but it also successfully fostered collaboration and peer mentoring, both valuable skills. In each pair of participants, one was designated the navigator and the other was driver to help divide the effort. Pairs were encouraged to switch partway through the program to experience different parts of the work. The kids tended to ask each other for help and work out any bugs together before asking the librarian or teen mentor-in-training for help, which gave the kids more confidence and ownership of the project, especially when it came time to show off their custom game to families and other participants at the end of the program.

To attract a diverse group of kids, the program, and supporting elements, purposely included a team of three female, multigenerational mentors, and a variety of projects and tools. Women and girls are often underrepresented in coding and gaming programs, but this strategy worked, and the group of kids included both genders and reflected the community's variety of cultural experiences.

Future Plans

The success of this initiative has spurred both interest in game design and coding among kids at the library and a willingness among library staff and decision makers to offer similar, more in-depth programs for kids ages 8 to 13. Expanding on the one-off workshop, a four-week program on video game design is being planned for the summer.

SOURCE: Claudia Haines, Homer (Alaska) Public Library

TEEN MEDIA MENTOR INTERN PROGRAM

The internship program trains teens in video and music production at the Studio i space so they can mentor their peers and create high-quality content to represent ImaginOn programs.

Target audience:	Ages 13–18
Participant number:	6–12 interns per session
Media used:	Software such as Pinnacle, GarageBand, iMovie, Final Cut, Scratch, and Stop Motion Pro; equipment such as computers, cameras, sound recording equipment, and blue screens
Staff involvement:	1 teen librarian and 5 other ImaginOn staff
Experience required:	Creating content with a variety of video and audio recording equipment, managing teens
Costs:	Staff time (all equipment is already part of Studio i)
Funding:	Charlotte Mecklenburg Library (library staff)
Partner organizations:	Charlotte Mecklenburg Library and Children's Theatre of Charlotte
Community size:	990,000 (Charlotte, North Carolina)
Duration:	4-month internships, offered 3 times a year

ImaginOn blends a library and theatre into one innovative space. The collaboration takes the best of both entities and uses combined resources to offer creative programs and learning experiences for all ages. Within the ImaginOn building, teens will find a space just for them. The Loft is a teen-specific area that includes Studio i, where video, animation, and music come to life. Teens and their families can create stories using digital tools and then take them home on a disc or upload them to the ImaginOn's YouTube playlist.

The ImaginOn intern program aims to develop local teens' digital literacy skills and provide additional tech support for teens and their families visiting the space. Teen interns use their new skills to create projects of their own as well as video tutorials, music videos, animated videos, and promos for upcoming ImaginOn events. Other teens record podcasts and music in the sound booth. Once teens are trained to use all of the Studio i equipment, they become mentors for their peers, showing budding artists how to use the equipment and create their own stories. Interns are also trained to monitor the music being recorded so the creative juices keep flowing without sacrificing the family-friendly nature of the space.

Lessons Learned

The successful intern program was not particularly structured when it first began. That situation has changed, in part to allow staff to measure outcomes for evaluation purposes. For example, the program now includes an assessment tool in which the teen mentors demonstrate their knowledge of a particular software. This assessment helps both staff and the teens themselves understand what they have learned during the internship.

Future Plans

Building on its popularity, Studio i space will integrate more makerspace-type activities and equipment so interns, as well as the other teens and families who visit the space, can work on a variety of projects in addition to the videos and music they have historically developed. The additional tools that teens will be able to use in the space include 3-D printers, sewing machines, and robots.

SOURCE: Kelly Czarnecki, ImaginOn / Charlotte Mecklenburg Library (North Carolina)

Access to Curated Media

CIRCULATING MAKER KITS

In addition to books, audiobooks, and other traditional library materials, a school library checks out librarian-created maker kits to provide access to new technology and content creation tools.

Target audience:	Ages 5–11
Participant number:	10–12 checkouts per month
Media used:	GoldieBlox blocks, Q-Ba-Maze blocks, paper circuits
Staff involvement:	1 school librarian, 1 assistant
Experience required:	Understanding basic electrical circuits, matching maker kit contents with academic standards
Costs:	$10–$32/kit
Funding:	School budget
Partner organizations:	Spring Ridge Elementary School only
Community size:	515 (students in school) plus 10,481 (Wyomissing, Pennsylvania)
Duration:	Ongoing

The school librarian is always looking for ways to engage kids (grades K–5) and help them meet academic standards. The librarian incorporates a variety of media, both high tech and low tech, into class visits and the items kids can check out. When classes visit the school library, they explore a variety of rotating centers focused on four areas—research, reading, language, and maker—before the weekly "book exchange," a time to check out library materials. Each center is aligned with an academic standard, making it easy for staff, administration, and parents to make the connection between the center activities and school objectives. As the school year unfolds, kids work through the research centers first and then move on to the other areas, acquiring badges (stickers) as they "level up," and other activities, like the maker centers, are "unlocked." The maker centers have included e-sewing with conductive materials, building with GoldieBlox blocks, and designing marble mazes with Q-Ba-Maze components.

Although the school has a one-to-one program (each child is issued a laptop for use at school and home) and the library has several Android tablets incorporated into daily use, the librarian wanted to provide access to other tools that encourage development of problem-solving skills, promote digital citizenship, and inspire kids to teach themselves and be lifelong learners. Without much space, maker kits were the ideal solution. Kids can check out the maker kits, which are based on center activities that the kids tried during their weekly library visit. Checking out the maker kits gives kids more time to tinker with the materials.

The three types of maker kits are kept in plastic media bags, much like a puzzle or other kit, and are easy to transport and manage. The following kits are available:

GoldieBlox: storybook plus building pieces (purchased set)

Marble Maze: Q-Ba-Maze modular blocks, marbles, and copied, laminated instruction sheets (two kits are made from one purchased set)

Paper Circuits: copper tape, LED lights, coin cell battery, paper, Nursery Rhyme story sheets, and laminated instructions with a QR code to the library's website (supplies are purchased separately and then made into kits)

When the barcoded, cataloged kits are returned to the library, the librarian or assistant can easily check what should be in the kit using the inventory list on the outside of the bag and replace any consumables (Paper Circuits kit).

Lessons Learned

The most popular take-home maker kits were featured as library centers. Many of the kids are more apt to play with the materials in the kit if they have used or seen them before. In fact, some of the kits were made because the activity time during the forty-minute library visits was too short to fully explore the center (e-sewing, for example). The library allows a five-item checkout limit to make sure kids can check out a popular maker kit *and* books instead of having to choose one or the other.

Future Plans

The librarian plans to make additional circulating maker kits based on success-ful library centers as time allows. Two kits currently being developed will allow kids to tinker with e-sewing (sewing with conductive materials) and stop-motion animation.

SOURCE: Collette Jakubowicz (A Wrinkle in Tech [blog]), Spring Ridge Elementary School (Wyomissing, Pennsylvania)

LISTENING STATION

A need to maintain a successful service and update technology transforms a CD-player-based listening station into one using an iPad.

Target audience:	Ages 8 and under and their families
Participant number:	5–10 listeners per day (in the first two months of use there were 1,516 read-alouds)
Media used:	iPad, 20 audiobooks from iTunes, multiple copies of paper books (same titles as audiobooks), peripherals (Archelon EXO Wall Mount, Califone mini stereo jackbox, Anchors [under-desk headphone hangers])
Staff involvement:	1 librarian
Experience required:	Using an iPad; finding, evaluating, and downloading high-quality digital audiobooks; troubleshooting technical issues
Costs:	$900
Funding:	Friends of the Bedford (Massachusetts) Free Public Library
Partner organizations:	Bedford Free Public Library and the Friends of the Bedford Free Public Library
Community size:	14,000 (Bedford, Massachusetts)
Duration:	Ongoing

The library's children's area featured a well-loved listening station that included an out-of-date CD player, and library staff needed new tools to provide families access to audiobooks in the library. The library already had mounted iPads for families to use, and the staff figured out how to adapt the iPad to improve a popular service.

The iPad is mounted in the heart of the children's library on a wall near an existing outlet. Two kids or a child and an adult can listen together thanks to four headsets, a splitter, and two comfortable chairs. The children's librarian finds, evaluates, and downloads the digital audiobooks from Apple's iBooks and pairs them with multiple copies of matching paper books so kids and families can listen and follow along in the paper book if they want. The same twenty books stay on the iPads for extended periods so there is minimal staff maintenance. The combination of space design, technology, and high-quality content all encourage joint media engagement—just what the librarian intended.

Related Program—Mounted iPads. When the library staff added mounted iPads to the library space, they wanted to make sure the families' experience was about media mentorship and learning. Alongside the iPads, families find information about joint media engagement, high-quality apps, and use of digital media with kids. The access and the mentorship proved to be valuable experiences for kids and adults alike. Library staff then evaluated the mounted iPad access project when they considered how to make the listening station successful.

Lessons Learned

The one technical difference that staff found between the CD player and the iPad was the ability to make sure that the downloaded books don't get deleted from the device and that the settings programmed by library staff are maintained for consistent performance. Library staff turned to the ALSC electronic discussion list for help. One suggestion has worked—the iPad's feature called Guided Access locks the user into a particular app and requires a passcode to turn off. This ability was what staff needed to prevent book deletions and settings changes. Although the iPad was not designed to be a listening station at a public library, the library staff were able to tinker with the device and some of its features to provide access to high-quality content, replace an outdated tool, and expose families to a popular digital device.

Future Plans

The library plans to integrate more new media into library services and programs. Next, the library plans to provide access to Playaway Launchpads, a different type of tablet, for checkout.

SOURCE: Bethany Klem, Bedford (Massachusetts) Free Public Library

CHICAGO PUBLIC LIBRARY YOUMEDIA

YOUmedia connects young adults, books, digital media, mentors, and institutions throughout Chicago in innovative learning spaces designed to inspire collaboration and creativity.

Target audience:	Ages 11–14 (middle-school sites)
Participant number:	10,272 visits at the four sites for middle schoolers in 2015
Media used:	Computers; video game consoles; cameras; recording equipment and software; fabric; printmaking, painting, and drawing supplies; paper books in the closely associated library collections
Staff involvement:	In addition to the teen services staff at each branch, a multiyear grant funds 2–3 additional part-time specialists at the YOUmedia sites plus a small group of YOUmedia project administrators
Experience required:	General understanding of how to use a variety of digital media tools plus a special interest (writing, music production, video, graphic design, etc.)
Costs:	Undisclosed
Funding:	Multiyear MacArthur Foundation grant through Chicago Public Library Foundation and Chicago Public Library / City of Chicago
Partner organizations:	Chicago Public Library (CPL) and YOUmedia Network
Community size:	2,695,598 (Chicago, Illinois)
Duration:	Year-round, after-school programming

Inspired by the work of cultural anthropologist Mizuko Ito, CPL staff set out to create a space where teens (ages 12–18) would feel comfortable and have the resources for "hanging out, messing around, and geeking out." Ito's research found that when teens are doing these three things, important learning happens. At Chicago Public Library's locations, that concept looks like an intentionally designed space with high-quality traditional and digital tools, library staff and mentors with a variety of digital media expertise, and the opportunity to learn informally about topics that interest individual teens at a personalized pace.

The CPL-funded librarians and grant-funded mentors provide workshop experiences, but much of the inspired learning and creating happens when teens find something they're interested in. The teens explore, play, design, and create on their own or in small groups with the help of librarians and mentors. Teens are using the on-hand tools to create music, poetry, screen prints, and movies, and YOUmedia offers multiple opportunities for the teens to show-case their work.

The libraries with YOUmedia spaces were selected with equity in mind. They are geographically distributed throughout the city to make it easy for teens citywide to access a space—for example, after school on public transportation. Word of mouth has been the best marketing tool, so when teens can easily access the spaces, more teens are likely to join them.

Related Program—Teen Mentors. YOUmedia Chicago recently started a teen alumni mentors program that connects teens who have been part of the YOU-media experience with new teens, at the Harold Washington Library Center in particular. CPL hopes to expand the mentorship program to connect teen alumni with more of the spaces, including the locations for younger, middle-school-age teens.

Lessons Learned

Staffing at the YOUmedia locations includes a mix of both CPL teen librarians and community members who are hired on as (grant-funded) specialists with some sort of digital media expertise. This approach has worked well and has allowed the program to incorporate mentors who complement the library staff and bring value to the teens' experiences.

Future Plans

In response to the success of the YOUmedia sites, CPL hopes to expand beyond the current twelve locations as resources allow. In the short term, CPL is looking at ways to develop the YOUmedia culture in other branches through professional development and by shared use of equipment and staff.

SOURCE: Julie Koslowsky, YOUmedia Outreach Coordinator for Chicago Public Library / Advanced Resources LLC (Illinois)

MAKER JAWN

A cross-generational, system-wide program provides access to digital and traditional tools as well as the expertise of community mentors to help families, kids, and teens explore, learn, and create.

Target audience:	Ages 6–14 and their families
Participant number:	7,519 at all sites (2015)
Media used:	Computers, 3-D printers, cameras, sewing machines, cardboard, a variety of other high- and low-tech tools
Staff involvement:	1 or 2 part-time mentors (not library staff) for each of 6 sites
Experience required:	Familiarity with a variety of low- and high-tech maker tools and demonstrated interest in working with community members.
Costs:	Undisclosed
Funding:	Institute of Museum and Library Services grant, Free Library of Philadelphia, Curiosity Creates grant (ALSC)
Partner organizations:	Free Library of Philadelphia and the Free Library of Philadelphia Foundation
Community size:	1,553,000 (Philadelphia, Pennsylvania)
Duration:	Year-round after-school and weekend programming

Born from computer hot spots operated by digital resource specialists, Maker Jawn has evolved since 2013 into makerspaces that encourage creativity and media literacy with a variety of high- and low-tech tools. The six sites are now run by maker mentors hired for their interest, expertise, and enthusiasm for science, technology, engineering, art, and math. Mentors, considered a key to Maker Jawn's success, expose kids, teens, and their families to materials, tools, skills, and activities in informal learning spaces, building relationships and inspiring exploration.

The everyday activities are made available in low-pressure experiences, allowing skills to develop at personalized paces and often as a result of failures or mistakes, an important aspect of experimentation. Kids and teens experiment with cardboard, animation, 3-D printing, kinetic sculptures, sewing, and video newscasts. Mentors also provide special workshops at the individual sites, many of which are located at library branches in neighborhoods challenged by poverty and where access to new media and makerspaces is extremely limited. Work is celebrated with displays at the different sites and a new digital badging system that recognizes the young makers' accomplishments.

Lessons Learned

Although Maker Jawn was inspired by programs like YOUmedia in Chicago, staff felt it was important to develop a project and spaces that are specific to local needs and resources. Understanding the project's audience members, what they need and want, is vital.

There is some turnover among the grant-funded, part-time mentor staff (not library staff), which can be challenging. Mentors often include artists, local college students, and other community members who may need training and extra support in managing kids at the Maker Jawn sites. To deal with these challenges, a city position was created to specifically oversee the mentors.

Future Plans

To involve more families, Maker Jawn sites plan to offer more weekend hours that will provide better access for working caregivers and teens who may have family responsibilities after school. The project will also continue to search for sustainable funding beyond the grants staff have secured to successfully launch and expand the program thus far.

SOURCE: Theresa Ramos and Sarah Winchowky, Free Library of Philadelphia Foundation (Pennsylvania), K-Fai Steele, National Writing Project

ALSC WHITE PAPER

Media Mentorship in Libraries Serving Youth

Abstract

The number of children and families who use digital media is growing, and children require mediated and guided experiences with digital media for the experiences to translate into positive and productive digital literacy skills. Libraries have the capacity to support families with all their literacy needs, traditional and digital, including needs as they arise. Librarians and youth services staff support children and their families in their decisions and practice around media use. Library staff serving youth and families embrace life-long learning, take advantage of training programs, and create opportunities to develop media mentor skills. It is the responsibility of library training programs, including library schools and formal professional development opportunities, to prepare future and current librarians and youth services practitioners to serve as media mentors. It is the responsibility of supervisors, administrations, and professional associations to support practitioners in this capacity.

Background

Libraries serving children and their families serve ever-evolving roles. In the contemporary youth services landscape, families engage in media in a variety of formats: print books, the bread and butter of our collections; audiobooks

Written for the Association for Library Service to Children by Amy Koester, Claudia Haines, Dorothy Stoltz, and Cen Campbell

Adopted by the ALSC Board of Directors on March 11, 2015

and audiovisual materials; and, most recently, digital media. As the materials and services required by the families we serve change and expand, our core functions as practitioners serving youth change and expand as well. This premise of providing responsive and essential services is built into ALSC's *Competencies for Librarians Serving Children in Public Libraries,* updated most recently in 2009. These core competencies assert the necessity of youth services staff regularly assessing community needs (I.3); responding to needs of the service population (I.6); creating and providing an environment that is both enjoyable and offers "convenient access to and use of library resources" (I.7); listening to children and families to ascertain their needs (III.2); and continually developing skills pertaining to technology and related tools (IX.2). All five of these competencies contribute to a central concept: that it is a fundamental responsibility of youth services staff to meet the needs of children and their families with regard to both access to and support of digital media, and to prioritize the development of our own knowledge of these areas so that we might best serve our communities.

There is little doubt that our communities are utilizing, and have personal interest in, digital media. *Digital media* refers predominantly to apps and e-books, but it may also include software programs as well as broadcast and streaming media. Typically, digital media involve one or more aspects of interactivity "designed to facilitate active and creative use by young children to encourage social engagement with other children and adults" (Schomburg and Donohue 2012, 1). In 2013, the most recent year for which Common Sense Media—one of the only organizations collecting and publishing data on children's digital media use—released statistics, 75 percent of households owned digital media in some format, up from 52 percent in 2011. Ownership of tablet devices, like iPads and similar touch screen devices, increased 500 percent in that same period, with 40 percent of families with children 8 or younger owning at least one such device in 2013. Additionally, in 2013, 72 percent of children ages 0 to 8 had used digital media of some kind (Rideout 2013; The Nielsen Company 2014). Use and exposure to digital media among children and families is both high and growing. Digital media is clearly highly relevant to the families we serve every day.

Even as families have increasing access to digital media, there remains a gap in families having information pertaining to how to utilize digital media and their supporting devices effectively and educationally (Vaala 2013). Digital literacy, as a result, is of tantamount importance. This need for services and collections that support the development of digital literacy fits squarely within the purview of library services for children and their families. Indeed, the programming and services for which libraries are most well-known have historically supported specific literacy needs among the service population. According to Nelson and Braafladt (2012), "Story times were never about teaching kids to read; rather they were developed to expose them to literacy practices in a safe setting and with a wider array of tools than most families could provide" (8).

There is precedent for libraries creating and tailoring programming and services to best meet the needs of the children and families they serve, and this relatively newer need for digital literacy is no different. It follows that libraries, in fulfilling their charge, support young children and families in this digital landscape to the best of our abilities.

Yet when it comes to supporting families in a world of tablets, apps, and interactive ebooks, libraries providing access to the media and relevant equipment is not, in and of itself, enough. Access alone is insufficient for facilitating children's positive and fruitful experiences with digital media; there also needs to be a degree of both regulation and modeling of use by adult caregivers for the digital media experience to be productive (Takeuchi 2011). Access to media only provides children exposure to certain functionalities of the media and platforms. Yet even this exposure may itself be inherently limited, as technology and media of any type may not be fully accessible to children if there is no caregiver positioned to provide guidance (Daugherty, Dossani, Johnson, and Oguz 2014). If a child requires the instruction of an adult in order to use digital media appropriately and effectively, then mounting an iPad in the youth department alone does little to develop the digital literacy skills of the children who attempt to use it.

Children require mediated and guided experiences with digital media for the experiences to translate into positive and productive digital literacy skills; this requirement holds true across a wide age range of youth. Children who are less likely to have direct adult or caregiver guidance when using digital media, and the Internet in particular, tend to "spend more time on lower-quality Web sites or activities that won't help them develop school-based skills" (Gutnick et al. 2011, 22), regardless of how much time a child spends with the media.

Quantity of exposure is no substitute for the quality of experiences. High-quality experiences with media of all types are not limited to supporting digital literacy skills development, however; rich experiences also support development of other core literacies, including social-emotional literacy and media literacy, both of which are integral for youth to succeed as both students and eventual members of the workforce (The Aspen Institute Task Force on Learning and the Internet 2014). Naidoo (2014) indicates that digital media experiences can be used to foster global understanding and empathy as well as cultural competence, which contribute to social-emotional literacy. Media literacy, too, is a vital component of twenty-first-century skills, and "technology-infused programs for older youth, then, are simply storytimes for the twenty-first century—exposing kids to key literacy skills at a critical time in their lives" (Nelson and Braafladt 2012, 9). Positive digital media experiences can support the educational and literacy development of children in myriad ways, a fact with which caregivers seem familiar.

In the report *Learning at Home,* Rideout (2014) reported that 57 percent of parents claim their children have gained knowledge in a particular subject through use of educational media. These parents see the potential for positive uses of media, yet only 44 percent of survey participants considered their children's screen media use to be educational. There seems to be a gap between what caregivers see as the potential positive benefits of digital media, and their ability to support their children in using said media most effectively. That gap is the perfect place for the library to step in with knowledge, modeling, and support.

To be clear, although digital media and tablet technology are still relatively new—the iPad debuted in 2010—there does exist a significant pool of knowledge about children's use of digital media. The American Academy of Pediatrics (AAP) has been making recommendations pertaining to children's media use the longest, with more than thirty years' worth of evolving positions. The AAP Council on Communications and Media released their most recent statement in 2013, at which point they offered a number of recommendations, including

- that health-care providers educate themselves on topics pertaining to media;
- that well-child visits include questions regarding a child's daily recreational screen time and whether the child has a television or device with Internet access in the bedroom;
- that caregivers limit children's entertainment screen time to less than one to two hours daily;
- that children under the age of two should not be exposed to screen media;
- that caregivers monitor their children's media use, both in terms of time spent with media and the types of media being accessed; and
- that caregivers establish a family media plan.

This 2013AAP position statement differed from its predecessors in the recommendations that well-child visits include discussion of media use and that families create media plans, but a number of health professionals responded that the crux of the position remained too much the same as previous incarnations. Rich (2014) asserts that the AAP statement relies too heavily on potential negative effects of screen use at the expense of fully considering positive and prosocial uses; he argues that this reliance on negative effects reduces the resonance of the AAP position with parents, many of whom feel their children are not susceptible to the potential serious and long-term detrimental effects of media use. Christakis (2014), on the other hand, takes issue with the AAP's unchanging recommendation of no screen time for children under age two, as well as their static definition of screen time. Christakis proffers that touch screen devices require their own recommendations separate from traditional screen media (i.e., television) because of their reactivity, interactivity, tailorability, portability, and facilitation of joint engagement. New digital media, Christakis asserts, is fundamentally different from the type of screen time about which the AAP has been advising for decades, and as such requires new and unique recommendations. Radesky, Schumacher, and Zuckerman (2015) share this position, citing the interactive aspects of media in their call for further research on young children and media. The trio also argues that families require media guidance even amidst ongoing research. They specifically recommend that caregivers be encouraged to try a technology before allowing their children to use it, and they also advise that caregivers engage in technology use with their children.

In 2012, the National Association for the Education of Young Children (NAEYC) and the Fred Rogers Center for Early Learning and Children's Media released a joint position statement that has widely been considered the counterpoint to the AAP position (Schomburg and Donohue 2012). This joint statement begins deliberately with a definition of interactive media and its difference from traditional, passive screen media, a point that Christakis (2014) argues the AAP should also make. Ultimately, Schomburg and Donohue (2012) declare that "technology and interactive media are tools that can promote effective learning and development when they are used intentionally by early childhood education, within the framework of developmentally appropriate practice, to support learning goals established for individual children" (5). This position is transformational, acknowledging that positive uses exist for young children and digital media when those media are utilized and moderated by an adult caregiver in ways that are intentional, appropriate, and relevant to the child using the media. These caveats for positive use mirror the concept of the "three C's" offered by Guernsey (2012); she asserts that any discussion of media use with children cannot be separate from also discussing the content of the media, the context in which it is being used, and the individual child who is engaging in the media experience.

In addition to considering the individual circumstances of digital media use by children, how and with whom the device is used are also important factors. This concept, termed *joint media engagement,* is defined as "spontaneous and designed experiences of people using media together" (Takeuchi and Stevens 2011, 10). This practice of interacting with media together allows the experience itself, as well as the content of the media, to resonate more deeply with the child using it. This resonance is especially true for young children jointly engaging with media with an adult caregiver, where the caregiver can use their knowledge and access to additional materials or spaces to extend the activities or concepts from the media beyond that media (e.g., arranging a walk in a park as an extension of a shared media experience pertaining to autumn leaves). Recent guidelines from Zero to Three reiterate the positive effects of joint media engagement (Lerner and Barr 2014), emphasizing the necessity of caregivers participating in screen use, making that use interactive, and extending the content beyond the screen to maximize learning. Daugherty, Dossani, Johnson, and Wright (2014) assert that these metrics—how and with whom the technology is being used and what the content offers—are more important in evaluating children's media use and habits than considering screen time alone.

Additional research exists beyond these formal position statements. With regard to potential educational aspects of digital media and its ability to positively impact children who engage with it, touch screen technology allows children to learn through hands-on experience, offering "a mode of interactive experience that mirrors the children's natural constructivist learning" (U.S. Department of Education and Michael Cohen Group 2012, 2). Similarly, app design has been shown to be a factor in educational impact. With book apps in particular, steady pacing, few distractions, and limited sound effects or games correlate to greater positive effects of app use (Parish-Morris et al. 2013). Furthermore, apps and digital games with multiplayer capabilities have been shown to support prosocial development, with students playing together presenting better social skills than solitary players (Takeuchi and Vaala 2014). Research also indicates some of the potential negative effects of poor media-use habits, in particular with regard to heavy use at the expense of other, nondigital media experiences. Constant exposure to and use of digital media may affect children's ability to properly interpret social cues in face-to-face interactions (Uhls et al. 2014), a fact that is potentially troubling considering caregivers are less likely to impose restrictions on the quantity of time spent engaging with media than they are to restrict types of media (Rideout, Foehr, and Roberts 2010).

Amidst these existing position statements and research findings, it is worthwhile to consider how libraries are currently responding to this changing digital landscape. A 2014 survey by ALSC, LittleeLit.com, and the iSchool at the University of Washington aimed to understand a piece of that landscape, honing in on new media use with young children. The study found that, of the 415 individual libraries and library systems that participated in the survey (ranging in legal service-area population from fewer than 5,000 customers to more than one million customers), 71 percent reported new media use in some capacity in programming and services for young children. The most frequent types of tablet utilization were offering tethered devices for young children in the library (40 percent of respondents) and using devices as part of storytime programming (39 percent of respondents). Libraries also indicated making devices available for checkout and use both inside and out of the library. Ninety libraries, or 22 percent of the survey population, reported providing device mentoring services (Mills et al., forthcoming).While this data regarding device use and tablet ownership resembles the 2013 Common Sense

Media family media-use data, the comparatively small number of libraries currently offering device mentorship in any capacity would seem to be the area primed for growth.

In 2014, Lisa Guernsey, director of the New America Foundation's Early Education Initiative, gave a TEDx talk in which she proposed, "What if we were to commit to ensure that every family with young children had access to a media mentor? This could be someone like a children's librarian." With this suggestion, Guernsey ushered in the idea of youth services library staff as a fundamental resource and support in the digital lives and decisions of the families we serve.

Considering the potential positive outcomes for children engaging with developmentally appropriate media, the goal of supporting families in creating a realistic media diet is a worthy one (Vossen, Piotrowski, and Valkenburg 2015). Indeed, the AAP's call for families to develop a family media plan implies just that—that setting intentional and appropriate parameters for family media use is positive and recommended (2013). It is within the capacity of youth services practitioners in particular to take on this role of media mentors; we are already expected to be familiar with child development, to support families in their information seeking, and to keep abreast of developments that pertain to and impact the families we serve (Association for Library Service to Children 2009). Embracing media mentorship simply incorporates a highly relevant and responsive service into our fundamental dedication to serving the children and families in our communities where they are, to the best of our abilities, and regardless of the format of preferred material. Indeed, this role is a worthwhile and needed one, in particular regard to digital media; research indicates the huge potential impact of youth services librarians filling this role: "Teachers, childcare providers, and families could benefit from seeing both appropriate and inappropriate practices in action" (Daugherty, Dossani, Johnson, and Wright 2014, 6). The needs of the children and families we serve—both spoken and implicit—and the fundamental role of librarians and youth services staff as resource and support for these children and families situate our profession to serve our communities in the capacity of media mentor.

Position

Taking into account the core functions of library services for youth, the evolving digital landscape, and children's and families' needs for support and resources, the following is recommended:

- Every library has librarians and other staff serving youth who embrace their role as media mentors for their community.
- Media mentors support children and families in their media use and decisions.

- Library schools provide resources and training to support future librarians and youth services practitioners in serving as media mentors.
- Professional development for current librarians and youth services practitioners include formal training and informal support for serving as media mentors.

In their report *Growing Young Minds,* the Institute for Museum and Library Services (IMLS) asserted the vital role of libraries as centers for providing families support and access to media of all kinds (Howard 2013). As "important community digital hubs, with expertise promoting digital, media, and information literacy" (22), libraries have already assumed an informal role in providing children and their families with access to and experiences in the digital landscape. With the IMLS recommending that federal and state policy makers, communities, schools, families, and funders better utilize the capacity of libraries to support children's learning, libraries can transform current informal access and experiences into full-fledged, robust support for families. By supporting librarians and other staff to embrace their role as media mentors, libraries are ensuring that they are equipped to support the developing and evolving needs of youth and families. A commitment to media mentorship in every library is a firm commitment to the full spectrum of being a supporter and champion of literacy.

Media mentors support children and their families in their decisions and practice around media use. This role encompasses a variety of strategies for support, with each child or family requiring individual mentoring to ensure that support is respectful, appropriate, and relevant.

The fundamental role of media mentors, according to Guernsey, is to assist families to "make choices about media and learn to use that media in developmentally appropriate ways" (as cited in Jackson 2014). A foundational aspect of this type of support is having access to and sharing recommendations for and research on children's media use from established medical, educational, and institutional sources. A media mentor provides recommendations to meet a family's stated or implied needs based on authoritative recommendations. A family looking for recommendations will be given these resources with objective interpretation by the media mentor, and it is up to the family to use the recommendations to make their own decisions regarding media use. As each family is different, so, too, will their media-use choices and habits be different—from eschewing all screen time to extensive media use, and everything in between.

In addition to providing access to and knowledge of media recommendations and research, media mentors provide opportunities "to help young children navigate, filter, and learn from the teeming media around them" (Guernsey 2013b). Media mentors actively engage with children and families interacting with digital media provided within the library context, both guiding children through positive and efficient uses of the technology and modeling for caregivers how they can support their children's digital literacy development outside of the library. Once families have made their media-use decisions, media mentors support those decisions to the best of their abilities. This level of support may include providing access to technology; offering programming with intentional technology use and related digital literacy learning experiences and information; and any other activities that support children and their families in using the technology they choose to use as appropriately and educationally as possible.

In order for every librarian and library staff serving youth to act as a media mentor, it is integral that library training programs adequately prepare future librarians and youth services practitioners to serve in this capacity. As "a well-trained facilitator is one of the most important determinants of whether technology use will result in skill growth" (Daugherty, Dossani, Johnson, and Oguz 2014, 16), future librarians and youth services staff require robust and comprehensive training in order to best support children and families in their digital literacy development. Library training programs, in particular library schools, should ensure future librarians and youth services practitioners have access to this training. Appropriate training includes full exploration of existing recommendations and research regarding children's media use; hands-on experience with digital media in both programmatic and one-on-one support settings; and resources for continued skill development and knowledge growth.

Librarians and youth services practitioners currently engaged in work in libraries also require training and support in order to fulfill their role as media mentors. It is essential that professional development opportunities, both formal and informal, include resources and support pertaining to this role. Formal professional development should include the same media-mentor training components as outlined for library schools: exploration of recommendations and research, hands-on experience, and resources for continued development. It is the responsibility of professional organizations, state libraries, and other established training providers to offer these formal professional development opportunities.

Librarians and youth services practitioners must be encouraged to develop their capacity as media mentors individually as well. This type of informal professional development should include identifying "trusted sources for resources and recommendations on technology and interactive media" (Donohue 2014, 6), including media evaluators such as librarians and reviewers; developing personal technology skills and digital media literacy; experimenting "with tools that enable children to create with old and new media" (Guernsey 2013a); and seeking out recent research on literacies, child brain development, and education. It is the responsibility of individual librarians and youth services practitioners, their supervisors, library administrations, and organizations setting standard competencies to recognize that media mentorship is a core function of serving youth and families, and to support development of media mentorship skills appropriately.

Conclusion

One of the strongest connections libraries have in the community is with children and families, and the children and families we serve are using digital media in increasing numbers. At the same time, many of these members of our communities lack the guidance and support to utilize such technology in ways that are ultimately productive, efficient, or educational for children. As an institution dedicated to supporting the rich literacy lives of our communities, and as professionals committed to the service of children and families, embracing and responding to this evolving landscape demonstrates our continued commitment to our communities' needs.

We must recognize the prevalence of media in the lives of our service populations and equip ourselves to best support them in their intentional, appropriate, and positive use of media. Librarians and youth services staff are embracing media mentorship in this capacity in order to serve families as they make their media decisions and develop digital and media literacy. This role as media mentor is a core function of supporting the lives and literacies of children and families in a twenty-first-century library. Equipping youth services practitioners to serve as media mentors is the shared responsibility of library training programs, creators of professional standards and professional development opportunities, and decision makers and practitioners at every level of library operations. With a strong commitment to media mentorship for youth and families, and to training youth services staff to be media mentors, libraries continue to fulfill their mission of supporting and meeting the needs of those we serve.

REFERENCES

American Academy of Pediatrics (AAP). 2013. "Have a Family Media Use Plan." AAP video, 1:01. https://www.aap.org/en-us/about-the-aap/aap-press-room/aap-press-room-media-center/Pages/Family-Media-Use-Plan.aspx.

American Academy of Pediatrics Council on Communications and Media. 2013. "Policy Statement: Children, Adolescents, and the Media." *Pediatrics* 132 (5): 958–61.

The Aspen Institute Task Force on Learning and the Internet. 2014. *Learner at the Center of a Networked World*. Washington, DC: The Aspen Institute.

Association for Library Service to Children. 2009. *Competencies for Librarians Serving Children in Public Libraries,* 3rd ed. Chicago: ALSC Education Committee.

Christakis, Dmitri A. 2014. "Interactive Media Use at Younger than the Age of 2 Years: Time to Rethink the American Academy of Pediatrics Guideline?" *JAMA Pediatrics* 168 (5): 399–400.

Daugherty, Lindsay, Rafiq Dossani, Erin-Elizabeth Johnson, and Mustafa Oguz. 2014. *Using Early Childhood Education to Bridge the Digital Divide.* Santa Monica, CA: RAND Corporation.

Daugherty, Lindsay, Rafiq Dossani, Erin-Elizabeth Johnson, and Cameron Wright. 2014. *Moving beyond Screen Time: Redefining Developmentally Appropriate Technology Use in Early Childhood Education.* Santa Monica, CA: RAND Corporation.

Donohue, Chip. 2014. "Early Learning in the Digital Age: What We Know and Why It Matters." *Early Childhood: The Newsletter of the Alliance for Early Childhood* 25 (2): 1–6.

Guernsey, Lisa. 2012. *Screen Time: How Electronic Media—From Baby Videos to Education Software—Affects Your Young Child.* Philadelphia: Basic Books.

Guernsey, Lisa. 2013a. "Early Learning in a Books Plus World: Rethinking Screen Time and Digital Media in Early Childhood." Presentation at the Head Start Birth-to-Five Leadership Institute, National Harbor, MD, April 29, 2013.

Guernsey, Lisa. 2013b. "iPads in the Classroom and Media Mentors." New American Foundation website blog. Accessed December 27, 2014. http://earlyed.newamerica.net/blogposts/2013/ipads_in_the_classroom_and_media_mentors-83299.

Guernsey, Lisa. 2014. "How the iPad Affects Young Children, and What We Can Do about It." TEDxMidAtlantic video, 13:14. Posted April 27, 2014. https://www.youtube.com/watch?v=P41_nyYY3Zg.

Gutnick, Aviva Lucas, Michael Robb, Lori Takeuchi, and Jennifer Kotler. 2011. *Always Connected: The New Digital Media Habits of Young Children.* New York: The Joan Ganz Cooney Center at Sesame Workshop.

Howard, Mary Lynn. 2013. *Growing Young Minds: How Museums and Libraries Create Lifelong Learners.* Washington, DC: Institute of Museum and Library Services.

Jackson, Sarah. 2014. "How Can Adults Help Young Children Learn from Screens?" *Remake Learning* (blog). Posted May 29, 2014. http://remakelearning.org/blog/2014/05/29/how-can-adults-help-young-children-learn-from-screens/.

Lerner, Claire, and Rachel Barr. 2014. *Screen Sense: Setting the Record Straight: Research-Based Guidelines for Screen Use for Children under 3 Years Old.* Washington, DC: Zero to Three.

Mills, J. Elizabeth, Emily Romeijn-Stout, Cen Campbell, and Amy Koester. "Results from the Young Children, New Media, and Libraries Survey: What Did We Learn?" *Children and Libraries* 13 (forthcoming).

Naidoo, Jamie Campbell. 2014. *Diversity Programming for Digital Youth: Promoting Cultural Competence in the Children's Library.* Santa Barbara: Libraries Unlimited.

Nelson, Jennifer, and Keith Braafladt. 2012. *Technology and Literacy: 21st Century Library Programming for Children and Teens.* Chicago: American Library Association.

The Nielsen Company. 2014. *The Digital Consumer.* New York: The Nielsen Company. www.nielsen.com/content/dam/corporate/us/en/reports-downloads/2014%20 Reports/the-digital-consumer-report-feb-2014.pdf.

Parish-Morris, Neha Mahajan, Kathy Hirsh-Pasek, Roberta Michnick Golinkoff, and Molly Fuller Collins. 2013. "Once Upon a Time: Parent-Child Dialogue and Story-book Reading in the Electronic Era." *Mind, Brain, and Education* 7 (3): 200–211.

Radesky, Jenny S., Jayna Schumacher, and Barry Zuckerman. 2015. "Mobile and Interactive Media Use by Young Children: The Good, the Bad, and the Unknown." *Pediatrics* 135 (1): 1–3.

Rich, Michael. 2014. "Moving from Child Advocacy to Evidence-Based Care for Digital Natives." *JAMA Pediatrics* 168 (5): 404–406.

Rideout, Victoria J. 2013. *Zero to Eight: Children's Media Use in America 2013.* Washington, DC: Common Sense Media.

Rideout, Victoria J. 2014. *Learning at Home: Families' Educational Media Use in America.* New York: The Joan Ganz Cooney Center at Sesame Workshop.

Rideout, Victoria J., Ulla G. Foehr, and Donald F. Roberts. 2010. *Generation M2: Media in the Lives of 8- to 18-Year-Olds.* Menlo Park, CA: Henry J. Kaiser Family Foundation.

Schomburg, Roberta, and Chip Donohue. 2012. *Technology and Interactive Media as Tools in Early Childhood Programs Serving Children from Birth through Age 8.* Washington, DC: National Association for the Education of Young Children and the Fred Rogers Center for Early Learning and Children's Media.

Takeuchi, Lori. 2011. "Kids Closer Up: Playing, Learning, and Growing with Digital Media." *International Journal of Learning and Media* 3 (2): 37–59.

Takeuchi, Lori, and Reed Stevens. 2011. *The New Coviewing: Designing for Learning through Joint Media Engagement.* New York: The Joan Ganz Cooney Center at Sesame Workshop.

Takeuchi, Lori, and Sarah Vaala. 2014. *Level Up Learning: A National Survey on Teaching with Digital Games.* New York: The Joan Ganz Cooney Center at Sesame Workshop.

Uhls, Yalda T., Minas Michikyan, Jordan Morris, Debra Garcia, Gary W. Small, Eleni Zgourou, and Patricia M. Greenfield. 2014. "Five Days at Outdoor Education Camp without Screens Improves Preteen Skills with Nonverbal Emotion Cues." *Computers in Human Behavior* 39 (Oct.): 387–92.

U.S. Department of Education and Michael Cohen Group. 2012. *Young Children, Apps, & iPad.* New York: U.S. Department of Education and Michael Cohen Group.

http://mcgrc.com/wp-content/uploads/2012/06/ipad-study-cover-page-report
-mcg-info_new-online.pdf.

Vaala, Sarah. 2013. *Aprendiendo Juntos (Learning Together): Synthesis of a Cross-
Sectorial Convening on Hispanic-Latino Families and Digital Technologies.* New York:
The Joan Ganz Cooney Center at Sesame Workshop.

Vossen, Helen G. M., Jessica Taylor Piotrowski, and Patti M. Valkenburg. 2015.
"Media Use and Effects in Childhood." In *The Handbook of Lifespan
Communication,* edited by J. F. Nussbaum, 93–112. New York: Peter Lang.

POSITION STATEMENTS AND KEY RECOMMENDATIONS
FOR CHILDREN AND NEW MEDIA

"Interactive Media Use at Younger than the Age of 2 Years: Time to Rethink the
American Academy of Pediatrics Guideline?" by Dimitri A. Christakis (2014),
http://archpedi.jamanetwork.com/article.aspx?articleid=1840251

*Moving beyond Screen Time: Redefining Developmentally Appropriate Technology Use
in Early Childhood Education,* by Lindsay Daugherty, Rafiq Dossani, Erin-
Elizabeth Johnson, and Cameron Wright, RAND Corporation (2014), www
.rand.org/content/dam/rand/pubs/research_reports/RR600/RR673z2/RAND
_RR673z2.pdf

The New Coviewing: Designing for Learning through Joint Media Engagement, by Lori
Takeuchi and Reed Stevens, The Joan Ganz Cooney Center at Sesame Workshop
(2011), www.joanganzcooneycenter.org/wp-content/uploads/2011/12/
jgc_coviewing_desktop.pdf

"Policy Statement: Children, Adolescents, and the Media," by American Academy of
Pediatrics Council on Communications and Media (2013), http://pediatrics
.aappublications.org/content/132/5/958.full

*Screen Sense: Setting the Record Straight: Research-Based Guidelines for Screen Use
for Children under 3 Years Old,* by Claire Lerner and Rachel Barr, Zero to Three
(2014), www.zerotothree.org/parenting-resources/screen-sense/screen-sense
_wp_final3.pdf

*Technology and Interactive Media as Tools in Early Childhood Programs Serving Children
from Birth through Age 8,* by Roberta Schomburg and Chip Donohue, National
Association for the Education of Young Children and the Fred Rogers Center for
Early Learning and Children's Media (2012), www.naeyc.org/files/naeyc/file/
positions/PS_technology_WEB2.pdf

RECOMMENDED READING

*Diversity Programming for Digital Youth: Promoting Cultural Competence in the
Children's Library,* by Jamie Campbell Naidoo. Santa Barbara: Libraries
Unlimited, 2014.

Screen Time: How Electronic Media—From Baby Videos to Education Software—Affects Your Young Child, by Lisa Guernsey. Philadelphia: Basic Books, 2012.

Technology and Digital Media in the Early Years: Tools for Teaching and Learning, edited by Chip Donohue. New York: Routledge, 2015.

Technology and Literacy: 21st Century Library Programming for Children and Teens, by Jennifer Nelson and Keith Braafladt. Chicago: American Library Association, 2012.

Young Children, New Media, and Libraries: A Guide for Incorporating New Media into Library Collections, Services, and Programs for Families and Children Ages 0–5, edited by Amy Koester. Evanston, IL: Little eLit, 2015. Available from http://littleelit.com/book/.

MEDIA EVALUATION RESOURCES

Children's Technology Review, http://childrenstech.com/

Digital-Storytime.com, http://digital-storytime.com/

The Horn Book's "App Review of the Week," www.hbook.com/category/choosing -books/app-review-of-the-week

School Library Journal's "Apps Reviews," www.slj.com/category/reviews/apps/#

Smart Apps for Kids, www.smartappsforkids.com

ABOUT THE AUTHORS

Cen Campbell is a children's librarian and the founder at LittleeLit.com. She has driven a bookmobile, managed branch libraries, developed innovative programs for babies, young children and teens, and now supports children's librarians to serve as media mentors in their communities. She was named Library Journal Mover & Shaker in 2014 for her work on LittleeLit.com.

Claudia Haines is the Youth Services Librarian at the Homer Public Library (Alaska). She designs and leads programs for young people ages eighteen and under and their families, provides community outreach, and manages the library's children and teen collections. She serves on both local and national committees that support early literacy and families, including the EMIERT Guidelines for Selecting Multicultural Materials Task Force. She provides training for other librarians using new media with young children and recently contributed to the book *Young Children, New Media, and Libraries: A Guide for Incorporating New Media into Library Collections, Services, and Programs for Families and Children Ages 0–5* (2015). She blogs at www.nevershushed.com.

Amy Koester is Youth & Family Program Coordinator at Skokie (IL) Public Library, where she coordinates programs for children through grade five and their families as well as man- ages fiction collections for youth and teens. She is editor of the book *Young Children, New Media, and Libraries: A Guide for Incorporating New Media into Library Collections, Services, and*

Programs for Families and Children Ages 0–5, and blogs regularly as the Show Me Librarian. Amy served on the 2014 Newbery Award Committee and is currently chair of the ALSC Public Awareness Committee.

Dorothy Stoltz coordinates programming and outreach services at Carroll County (MD) Public Library. She spearheaded a successful early literacy training study for Carroll using home child care providers and three and four year olds. She is co-author of several ALA Editions books, including, *Tender Topics: Picture Books about Life's Challenges (2013), The Power of Play: Designing Early Learning Spaces* (2015), and an upcoming book on early childhood collaborations. In 2011 she became a member of the ALSC/PLA Every Child Ready to Read Oversight Committee, and its chair for 2014–2015.

APPENDIX B

ALSC WHITE PAPER

The Importance of Diversity in Library Programs and Material Collections for Children

Abstract

Children encounter diversity on a regular basis in their interactions with others at home, in school, or around their neighborhood. As our nation continues to diversify, it is essential that children learn to understand the important role of their culture and the cultures of other people in creating an overall global culture respectful of differences. One way that children learn about the world around them and other cultures is through the social messages found in stories. Stories help children understand how society perceives their culture as well as the cultures of their classmates, teachers, caregivers, and others, thereby influencing their social and identity development. Stories can be found in traditional print materials for children or in newer digital formats. Regardless of the format for delivering a story's message, children are greatly influenced by the stories they encounter. One place that children can interact with stories on a regular basis is the library. Through its materials collections and programs, the library introduces children to many stories, starting at a very young age. This white paper emphasizes the importance of developing print and digital library collections that reflect cultural diversity, and details how librarians can promote cultural understanding through library programs that embody the diversity of their communities and the larger world. It concludes that stories reflecting diversity should be routinely included in library

Written for the Association for Library Service to Children by Jamie Campbell Naidoo, PhD

Adopted by the Association for Library Service to Children Board of Directors on April 5, 2014 programs throughout the year and represented in print and digital material collections and displays.

Background

Diversity in library collections and programs refers to cultural diversity. Culture includes shared characteristics that define how a person lives, thinks, and creates meaning. These characteristics include customs, traditions, rituals, food, dress, and language. Typically people from the same cultural group share similar characteristics. Nieto (1999) explains that the idea of culture is complex, extending beyond foods, festivals, fashion, and folklore to include daily experiences influenced by myriad social factors defined by a particular community or region as well as larger national influences. Ethnicity, race, family composition, ancestry, ability, sexual orientation, socioeconomic status, language fluency, citizenship status, religious preference, age, gender expression, education level, and domicile are all aspects of a person's culture. Children experience culture by way of their families' values and practices, in their daily interactions with others in school and throughout the community, and through the stories and characters they encounter in books, television programs and films, music, video and computer games, digital apps, and other forms of print and digital media.

In the field of sociocultural psychology, the work of Vygotsky (1986) informs us that language and culture play a significant role in a child's social and identity development and construction of meaning. Cultural traditions and social practices have the ability to moderate the way children think and learn. A child's self-esteem is largely influenced by the way the child and overall society views the cultural group to which the child belongs. Vygotsky explains that children use expressive media such as books to understand the world around them. Bishop (1997) also acknowledges the power of children's stories to influence a child's perception and suggests that children's literature can serve as a mirror reflecting a child's own life and culture, or as a window allowing children to peer into the lives of others. Books and other print and digital media convey to children how the world perceives people who are like them as well as people who are different. By the time they are toddlers, children have begun to develop a sense of self that is informed by the world around them (Hughes-Hassell and Cox 2010). Children's materials that accurately portray diversity in multiple languages and cultures can have a positive influence on a child's self-image and help him or her build bridges of cultural understanding. All children want to see images that reflect themselves and encounter stories in their native language and within the context of their personal cultures. Diverse, culturally authentic materials in library collections allow all children to meet people like themselves and develop an appreciation for the beauty of their culture and the cultures of others. Children's book author and illustrator Christopher Myers observes that books can also serve as road maps leading children to their destinies. Through the stories they encounter, children develop "an atlas of their world, of their relationships to others, [and] of their possible destinations" (C. Myers 2014).

Children's materials that provide inaccurate, stereotyped depictions of diverse languages and cultures can equally influence children. If children are consistently exposed to books and other media that negatively represent their culture, then it is likely they will internalize these social messages and develop a poor sense of self. Similarly, negative images or misinformation about a particular cultural group reinforces stereotypes in children outside the culture (W. Myers 2014). Children's picture books are some of the earliest forms of media that teach children about diversity in the world. Social messages that young children glean from picture books will likely stay with them for the rest of their lives (Roethler 1998; Henderson 1991).

The absence of a child's culture from the stories in print and digital media can also be problematic. When children never see their culture represented in a library storytime or in materials on the library shelves, they receive a resounding message that the librarian does not think their culture is important enough to feature in the library. This invisibility within the library's programs and materials can equally be harmful to a child's self-image. Latina children's book author and illustrator Maya Christina Gonzalez recalls that as a young child she felt lost in the library among the rows of books that reflected the lives of other children but not her Latino culture. Although she would often draw herself on the inside covers of her coloring books, she still did not feel important because there were no "real" hardcover library books depicting her experiences (2011). The problem of cultural invisibility or the lack of diversity in children's materials is a long-standing one. In 1941, Charlemae Hill Rollins observed that few children's books depicting African Americans were available and those that were accessible contained numerous harmful stereotypes. Later in 1965, Nancy Larrick reemphasized the lack of diversity in children's books in her seminal article "The All-White World of Children's Books," which chastised publishers for not publishing more books about African Americans. Afterwards, the Council on Interracial Books for Children (CIBC) began publishing additional reports highlighting the paucity of books representing African Americans, Latinos, Asian Americans, American Indians, people with disabilities, and gays and lesbians. In 1980, CIBC published a series of guidelines, *Ten Quick Ways to Analyze Children's Books for Sexism and Racism,* that are still used by librarians today to evaluate diversity in children's books. In the 1990s, more books representing cultural diversity began to appear in the United States, but compared to the overall number of books published each year, these books were greatly outnumbered by books representing White middle-class families. In 2014, Christopher Myers described this "All-White World" as "apartheid in literature," where stories about people of color (and other minorities) are relegated to townships, while stories about animals and White characters compose the predominant world of children's literature.

Every year since 1994, the Cooperative Children's Book Center at the University of Wisconsin–Madison has kept statistics on the number of children's books published about American Indians, Asian Americans, Latinos, and African Americans. In 1994, just over 8 percent of children's books published in the United States represented these populations. Twenty years later, this number is virtually the same, indicating that many children in the United States still do not have as many opportunities to see their cultures represented as White middle-class children do. As previously indicated, this lack of diversity in children's books can be harmful to the social and identity development of children, particularly those representing cultures with untold stories.

It is equally important for children to be exposed to library programs that highlight materials representing the diversity in languages and cultures present not only in their local community but also the larger world (Baker 1955; White 1964; Tate 1971; Larson 2011). Diversity in library programming allows children and their caregivers to develop cultural literacy, or an appreciation of their culture as well as the cultures of other people. Consistently offering programs that highlight cultural and linguistic diversity provides opportunities for children and their families to begin the journey to developing cultural competence, or the awareness of one's own culture and the contributions of other cultures, the ability to interact with other individuals from diverse cultures, and an understanding of how cultures are integrated together within our larger society (Montiel-Overall 2009). When children's librarians introduce diversity in materials and programming and promote cultural competence, they create learning environments that help children develop a positive sense of self, explore the larger world around them, and celebrate the accomplishments of people from diverse cultural and linguistic backgrounds.

One way to promote cultural competence in the library is through the literacy initiative El día de los niños/El día de los libros (Children's Day/Book Day), or Día for short. Developed in 1996 by Latina author Pat Mora along with founding partner REFORMA (The National Association to Promote Library and Information Services to Latinos and the Spanish-Speaking), Día is a family literacy program that uses libraries to connect children to books representing cultural and linguistic diversity. Housed at the Association for Library Service to Children (ALSC), a division of the American Library Association (ALA), Día emphasizes the importance of connecting all children from all cultural backgrounds with library materials in many languages about many cultures.

The goals of Día include celebrating children and connecting them to the world of learning through books, stories, and libraries; nurturing cognitive and literacy development in ways that honor and embrace a child's home language and culture; introducing families to community resources that provide opportunities for learning through multiple literacies; and recognizing and respecting culture, heritage, and language as powerful tools for strengthening families and communities (ALSC 2013). Día can be celebrated year-round with culminating events on April 30, the official day for celebrating children and books. Librarians who recognize Día as a daily commitment and incorporate its goals into their regular programming demonstrate their commitment to promoting diversity in library collections and programs.

Position

Recognized as trusted spaces that welcome children to explore, discover, and connect to the larger world, libraries can play an integral role in helping them develop understanding and respect for other people from diverse cultural and linguistic backgrounds. As our nation continues to diversify, it is essential that children learn to understand the important role of their culture and the cultures of other people in creating an overall global culture respectful of differences. By including diversity in its programs and collections, the library has the potential for helping children make cross-cultural connections and develop the skills necessary to function in a culturally pluralistic society.

Both the Institute of Museum and Library Services' *Growing Young Minds: How Museums and Libraries Create Lifelong Learners* (2013) and the Pew Research Center's *Parents, Children, Libraries, and Reading* (Miller et al. 2013) attest to the important role of the library as one of the first teachers of young children, delivering content-rich, age-appropriate early literacy programs and providing access to high-quality, engaging print and digital material collections. When libraries offer culturally authentic materials and displays, they convey the importance of using print and digital media to learn how different cultures share commonalities that make us very similar, but also have unique traits that enrich the world. By delivering culturally responsive programs such as Día, libraries (1) link home cultures with the larger social culture to promote traditional literacy; (2) provide an opportunity for silenced voices to be heard; (3) promote lifelong learning and achievement; (4) celebrate linguistic and cultural diversity; and (5) empower children to function in a global society (Diamond and Moore 1995).

An excellent way to build cultural bridges is to integrate authentic contemporary children's literature about diverse groups into library programs to promote cultural literacy and global understanding, thereby introducing children to the rich cultures of their peers, teachers, or future acquaintances (Moreillon 2013). Studies indicate that by preschool age, young children reveal stereotypes and negative behaviors towards those they perceive as different. These learned attitudes are fostered by the views of parents, caregivers, educators, and peers and by the social messages that reading materials convey about a particular culture. Librarians can help children develop favorable attitudes towards those perceived as the "other" by introducing them to authentic, high-quality literature about diverse cultures. Particularly, positive representations of diversity in children's materials

- provide positive role models for culturally diverse children;
- introduce children to characters with similar experiences and emotions;
- convey the richness and beauty of the diverse cultures in the United States;
- reinforce a distinct cultural identity;
- promote multilingual and literacy development;
- inspire learning of other cultures and general cultural knowledge;
- facilitate acceptance of cultures different from one's own; and
- foster global connections.

When selecting books for the library collection or to use in library programs, it is imperative that children's librarians choose materials representative of a wide range of perspectives and cultures. Opportunities should be provided for children and caregivers to hear stories and interact with characters whose lives and experiences are different from their own. Children need a global perspective on the world in order to develop cultural competence and move beyond their immediate environment. They need to hear more than one story once a year about a particular cultural group. Adichie (2009) warns that a single story can create or perpetuate stereotypes about a particular culture, offering children their only foray in the experiences of the "other" in society.

Librarians often rely on culturally generic books for storytime programs and exile cultural explorations to holidays and specialized heritage months: Black History Month, Chinese New Year, Native American Heritage Month, Hanukkah, Asian-Pacific American Heritage Month, Day of the Dead, and so on. If a child is only introduced to books about her culture one time a year, then she internalizes that the librarian thinks she or her culture is not important. What if this one-month venture into cultures includes materials that stereotype, demean, or provide misinformation? What is the culturally diverse child internalizing and what are her classmates learning about her culture? Even the highest quality materials and culturally authentic activities are irrelevant if children learn that their particular culture or the culture of their peers is not good enough to study or talk about throughout the year. While middle-class White children in heterosexual nuclear families have the opportunity to see their culture represented in library collections, programs, and displays on a daily basis, other children are lucky if they get their own special month or day. It is imperative that diversity be included in library programs and displays routinely throughout the year.

Similarly, if children are not exposed to the lives, cultures, and languages of children from around the world, they miss the opportunity to learn how to function in a culturally pluralistic world. Global understanding is part of being culturally competent. Children that exhibit global understanding can acknowledge how cultural differences, personal decisions, and social issues impact lives at a global level. At the same time, these children engage in local, national, or international social justice projects that reach out to their counterparts around the world. The road to developing global understanding and achieving cultural competence can start in the children's library by way of collections and programs that include cultural diversity.

Culturally responsive programs facilitate understanding and acceptance of diversity based upon culture, ethnicity, linguistic ability, religion, physical ability, immigration status, and sexual orientation. However, some librarians may not know how to offer these types of programs; instead they attempt to promote cultural competence and global understanding through a "tourist approach" common in many diversity-oriented library programs. This approach highlights the five Fs—foods, festivals, folklore, fashion, and famous people of a particular culture—rather than exploring the daily interactions of people within that culture. Ostensibly this practice may not seem objectionable, but it cannot be the only way to introduce and explore cultures in the library. Children need opportunities for meaningful engagement with cultures that are different from their own. Librarians have to be cautious when using the five Fs to avoid perpetuating cultural stereotypes and tokenism. Often this approach focuses on cultural elements that are exotic, flashy, or quaint. Introducing children to unusual fashion or "costumes" and festivals from a culture reinforces a sense of exoticism or otherness rather than fostering understanding. Only sharing folktales with children can give them a distorted view of a particular culture. When librarians rely on the five Fs to explore cultural diversity, it is extremely problematic if any of the Fs are not culturally accurate or reinforce outdated stereotypes. It is important for librarians to select materials that include books written and illustrated by people either from the culture being profiled or with considerable knowledge about and experience related to the culture. Librarians should examine the copyright date of the materials to identify outdated content. Some publishers of informational books will use the same photo in multiple editions of a book, only updating the narrative. This becomes problematic when a book meant to represent the contemporary lives of South Africans features photos taken before apartheid ended.

Culturally responsive library programs will introduce different cultures through quality children's materials (print and digital) and promote cross-cultural connections by inviting children to explore topics such as social justice, equality, and cultural authenticity. Culturally responsive programs provide a forum for examining issues of ethnicity, class, and culture. A library fully engaged in promoting cultural competence through collections and programs provides numerous opportunities for children and their families to learn about new cultures. Language is part of a child's culture. Libraries reinforce multilingualism by offering programs introducing children to a variety of languages and encouraging them to play with language acquisition. In a culturally competent library program, librarians share books and other materials about diverse cultures and introduce children to diverse languages through read-alouds in multiple languages, or songs designed to teach language learning.

Through cultural literacy initiatives such as Día, libraries have natural avenues for infusing cultural competence into their programs and services. Día allows libraries to build bridges between home cultures and languages and those of the school, library, larger community, and world. With its focus on celebrating diverse languages and cultures, Día provides a model for librarians interested in developing programs responsive to the needs of their local community. For programs to be successful, Garcia and Hasson (2004) note that librarians must design experiences that focus on the daily realities relevant to target populations. Librarians should keep in mind that particular populations or segments of their community may not readily have access to transportation to attend library programs. In these instances, librarians may want to develop outreach programs that propel the library into culturally diverse communities or partner with local community organizations currently serving these populations. Library programs should reflect the interests and goals of the target population. The most successful culturally responsive libraries involve diverse communities in the planning process, allowing them to assist in the materials selection, program development and delivery, and marketing. For years, public libraries have embraced Día as the cultural programming model for reaching culturally and linguistically diverse children and families. Día includes a diverse array of materials in multiple languages and about diverse cultures.

While the name *Día* is the Spanish word for *day*, Día can also stand for "Diversity in Action." When librarians embrace the charge of the literacy initiative to embody library programs that represent diversity in action, they understand that the principles of Día can be used throughout the year to promote cultural competence every day in library programs and collections. By making every day a Día day, librarians make a daily commitment to serving all children with resources and programs that foster global understanding, language learning, and cultural explorations. In doing so, libraries are able to deliver content-rich, age-appropriate early literacy programs for all children and provide access to high-quality, engaging print and digital material collections that help children develop a positive identity and make cultural connections.

Conclusion

Including diversity in library programming and materials for children is important for all librarians meeting the informational and recreational needs of their local communities. Children's print and digital materials should represent all types of diversity, including race, ethnicity, gender expression, religious preference, family composition, ancestry, ability, sexual orientation, socioeconomic status, language fluency, and citizenship status. More children's books representing diverse cultures should be made available to children through library collections to assist in their identity development and to help them make global connections.

Children and their families should be exposed to library programs throughout the year that celebrate cultural diversity and provide opportunities for developing bridges of understanding. The literacy initiative Día provides children's librarians with recommended materials and programming ideas for incorporating diversity into their daily library practices and emphasizes the library's commitment to serving all children from diverse cultural and linguistic backgrounds. Día offers library administrators and staff a replicable model, useful information, and invaluable resources to assist them in planning and developing culturally responsive and effective programs, collections, and services to meet the informational and recreational needs of their diverse communities.

References

Adichie, Chimamanda Ngozi. 2009. "The Danger of a Single Story." TED video, 18:49. Accessed Feb. 20, 2014. www.ted.com/talks/chimamanda_adichie_the_danger_of_a_single_story.html.

Association for Library Service to Children. 2013. "About Día" webpage. Accessed Feb. 28, 2014. http://dia.ala.org.

Baker, Augusta. 1955. "The Children's Librarian in a Changing Neighborhood." *Top of the News* 10 (Mar.): 40–41.

Bishop, Rudine Sims. 1997. "Selecting Literature for a Multicultural Curriculum." In *Using Multiethnic Literature in the K–8 Classroom,* edited by Violet Harris, 1–20. Norwood, MA: Christopher-Gordon Publishers.

Cooperative Children's Book Center. "Children's Books by and about People of Color Published in the United States." Annual Statistics. Accessed Mar. 6, 2014. http://ccbc.education.wisc.edu/books/pcstats.asp.

Council on Interracial Books for Children. 1980. *Ten Quick Ways to Analyze Children's Books for Sexism and Racism.* New York: Council on Interracial Books for Children.

Diamond, Barbara, and Margaret Moore. 1995. *Multicultural Literacy: Mirroring the Reality of the Classroom.* White Plains, NY: Longman.

Garcia, Delia, and Deborah Hasson. 2004. "Implementing Family Literacy Programs for Linguistically and Culturally Diverse Populations: Key Elements to Consider." *School Community Journal* 14 (1): 113–37.

Gonzalez, Maya Christina. 2011. "I Am All That I See: The Power of Reflection." In *Celebrating Cuentos: Promoting Latino Children's Literature and Literacy in*

Classrooms and Libraries, edited by Jamie Campbell Naidoo, 319–26. Santa Barbara, CA: Libraries Unlimited.

Henderson, Virginia M. 1991. "The Development of Self-Esteem in Children of Color." In *The Multicolored Mirror: Cultural Substance in Literature for Children and Young Adults,* edited by Merri V. Lindgren, 15–30. Fort Atkinson, WI: Highsmith Press.

Hughes-Hassell, Sandra, and Ernie J. Cox. 2010. "Inside Board Books: Representations of People of Color." *The Library Quarterly* 80 (3): 211–30.

Institute of Museum and Library Services. 2013. *Growing Young Minds: How Museums and Libraries Create Lifelong Learners.* Washington, D.C.: Institute of Museum and Library Services. PDF. Accessed Mar. 9, 2014. www.imls.gov/assets/1/AssetManager/GrowingYoungMinds.pdf .

Larrick, Nancy. 1965. "The All-White World of Children's Books." *Saturday Review* 11 (Sept.): 63–65.

Larson, Jeanette. 2011. "Building a Culture of Literacy through Día: Library Events Celebrate Bilingual Bookjoy." *American Libraries* (Mar./Apr.). Accessed Mar. 16, 2014. http://americanlibrariesmagazine.org/2011/03/22/building-a-culture-of-literacy-through-dia/.

Miller, Carolyn, Kathryn Zickuhr, Lee Rainie, and Kristen Purcell. 2013. *Parents, Children, Libraries, and Reading.* Pew Research Center's Internet & American Life Project. Accessed Mar. 8, 2014. http://libraries.pewinternet.org/2013/05/01/parents-children-libraries-and-reading/.

Montiel-Overall, Patricia. 2009. "Cultural Competence: A Conceptual Framework for Library and Information Science Professionals." *The Library Quarterly* 79 (2): 175–204.

Moreillon, Judi. 2013. "Building Bridges for Cultural Understanding: Cultural Literature Collection Development and Programming." *Children and Libraries* 11 (2): 35–38.

Myers, Christopher. 2014. "The Apartheid of Children's Literature." *New York Times,* Mar. 15. Accessed Mar. 17, 2014. www.nytimes.com/2014/03/16/opinion/sunday/the-apartheid-of-childrens-literature.html.

Myers, Walter Dean. 2014. "Where Are the People of Color in Children's Books?" *New York Times,* Mar. 15. Accessed Mar. 17, 2014. www.nytimes.com/2014/03/16/opinion/sunday/where-are-the-people-of-color-in-childrens-books.html.

Nieto, Sonia. 1999. *The Light in Their Eyes: Creating Multicultural Learning Communities.* New York: Teachers College Press.

Roethler, Jacque. 1998. "Reading in Color: Children's Book Illustrations and Identity Formation for Black Children in the United States." *African American Review* 32 (1): 95–105.

Rollins, Charlemae Hill, ed. 1941. *We Build Together: A Reader's Guide to Negro Life and Literature for Elementary and High School Use.* Urbana, IL: National Council of Teachers of English.

Tate, Binnie L. 1971. "The Role of the Children's Librarian in Serving the Disadvantaged." *Library Trends* 20 (Oct.): 392–404.

Vygotsky, Lev. 1986. *Thought and Language.* Cambridge, MA: MIT Press.

White, Pura Belpré. 1964. "A Bilingual Story Hour Program." *Library Journal* 89
(Sept. 15): 79–81.

Association for Library Service to Children (ALSC) Diversity Resources

"ALSC/Candlewick Press 'Light the Way: Outreach to the Underserved' Grant"
webpage, www.ala.org/alsc/awardsgrants/profawards/candlewicklighttheway

"Books on Islam for Children and Teens" webpage, https://alair.ala.org/
handle/11213/556.

El día de los niños/El día de los libros (Children's Day/Book Day) Diversity Initiative
website, http://dia.ala.org

"Growing Up around the World: Books as Passports to Global Understanding for
Children in the United States" webpage, www.ala.org/alsc/compubs/booklists/
growingupwrld/GrowingUpAroundWorld

Online Collection Development Resources

American Indians in Children's Literature blog, by Debbie Reese, http://
americanindiansinchildrensliterature.blogspot.com/

The Brown Bookshelf website, by Varian Johnson et al., http://thebrownbookshelf.com

CBC Diversity website, by Children's Book Council, http://www.cbcdiversity.com

De Colores: The Raza Experience in Books for Children blog, by Beverly Slapin et al.,
http://decoloresreviews.blogspot.com

Gay-Themed Picture Books for Children blog, by Patricia A. Sarles, http://
booksforkidsingayfamilies.blogspot.com/

International Children's Digital Library website, by the University of Maryland,
http://en.childrenslibrary.org

"Multicultural Reading" webpage, by Cynthia Leitich Smith, www.cynthialeitichsmith
.com/lit_resources/diversity/multicultural/multi_biblio.html

Awards for Culturally Diverse Children's Literature

American Indian Youth Literature Award, sponsored by the American Indian Library
Association, http://ailanet.org/activities/american-indian-youth-literature
-award/

Américas Book Award for Children's and Young Adult Literature (Latino literature), sponsored by the Consortium of Latin American Studies Programs, http://www4.uwm.edu/clacs/aa/index.cfm; http://claspprograms.org/pages/detail/37/Amricas-Book-Award

Arab American Book Award, sponsored by the Arab American National Museum, www.arabamericanmuseum.org/bookaward

Asian/Pacific American Award for Literature, sponsored by the Asian Pacific American Librarians Association, www.apalaweb.org/awards/literature-awards/

Carter G. Woodson Book Award (literature depicting ethnicity in the U.S.), sponsored by the National Council for the Social Studies, www.socialstudies.org/awards/woodson

Coretta Scott King Book Awards (African American literature), sponsored by the American Library Association's Ethnic and Multicultural Information Exchange Round Table (EMIERT), www.ala.org/ala/mgrps/rts/emiert/cskbookawards/index.cfm

Dolly Gray Children's Literature Award (literature depicting children with disabilities), sponsored by the Council for Exceptional Children's Division on Autism and Developmental Disabilities, http://daddcec.org/Awards/DollyGrayAwards.aspx

Jane Addams Children's Book Awards (literature promoting peace, social justice, world community, and equality of the sexes), sponsored by the Jane Addams Peace Association and the Women's International League for Peace and Freedom, www.janeaddamspeace.org/jacba/

Middle East Book Awards, sponsored by the Middle East Outreach Council, www.meoc.us/meoc/book-awards

Notable Books for a Global Society (global children's literature), sponsored by the International Reading Association, http://clrsig.org/nbgs.php

Outstanding International Books List, sponsored by the United States Board on Books for Young People, www.usbby.org/list_oibl.html

Pura Belpré Award (Latino literature), sponsored by the Association for Library Service to Children and REFORMA, www.ala.org/alsc/awardsgrants/bookmedia/belpremedal

Rainbow List (LGBTQ children's and young adult literature), sponsored by the American Library Association's Gay, Lesbian, Bisexual, and Transgender Round Table (GLBTRT), http://glbtrt.ala.org/rainbowbooks/

Schneider Family Book Award (literature about children with disabilities), sponsored by Katherine Schneider and the American Library Association, www.ala.org/awardsgrants/schneider-family-book-award

South Asia Book Award, sponsored by the South Asia National Outreach Consortium, www.sanoc.org/saba.html

Stonewall Children's and Young Adult Literature Award (LGBTQ literature), sponsored by the American Library Association's Gay, Lesbian, Bisexual, and Transgender Round Table (GLBTRT), www.ala.org/glbtrt/award

Sydney Taylor Book Award (Jewish literature), sponsored by the Association of Jewish Libraries, www.jewishlibraries.org/main/Awards/SydneyTaylorBookAward.aspx

Tomás Rivera Mexican American Children's Book Award, sponsored by Texas State University's College of Education, www.education.txstate.edu/c-p/Tomas-Rivera-Book-Award-Project-Link.html

Multicultural Children's Program Resources

¡Colorín Colorado! website, by Reading Rockets, www.colorincolorado.org

"Dai Dai Xiang Chuan: Bridging Generations, a Bag at a Time" webpage, by the Chinese American Librarians Association, http://daidai.cala-web.org

Lee y serás® (Read and You Will Be) website, by Scholastic, www.leeyseras.net

Noche de Cuentos website, by REFORMA (The National Association to Promote Library and Information Services to Latinos and the Spanish-Speaking), http://nochedecuentos.org

Programming Librarian website, by the American Library Association, www.programminglibrarian.org/home.html

"Reading Is Grand! Celebrating Grand-Families @ Your Library" webpage, by the Black Caucus of the American Library Association, http://bcalareadingisgrand.weebly.com

Talk Story: Sharing Stories, Sharing Culture website, by the American Indian Library Association and the Asian Pacific American Librarians Association, http://talkstorytogether.org

Professional Library Associations Dedicated to Culturally Diverse Groups

American Indian Library Association (AILA), www.ailanet.org

American Library Association's Ethnic and Multicultural Information Exchange Round Table (EMIERT), www.ala.org/ala/mgrps/rts/emiert/index.cfm

American Library Association's Gay, Lesbian, Bisexual, and Transgender Round Table (GLBTRT), www.ala.org/ala/mgrps/rts/glbtrt/index.cfm

Asian Pacific American Librarians Association (APALA), www.apalaweb.org

Association of Jewish Libraries (AJL), www.jewishlibraries.org/main

Black Caucus of the American Library Association (BCALA), www.bcala.org

Chinese American Librarians Association (CALA), www.cala-web.org

International Board on Books for Young People (IBBY), www.ibby.org

International Federation of Library Associations and Institutions (IFLA),
  www.ifla.org

REFORMA (The National Association to Promote Library and Information Services
  to Latinos and the Spanish-Speaking), www.reforma.org

AUTHOR'S NOTE: Jamie Campbell Naidoo is a current member of the ALSC
Board of Directors. The position, statements, and information provided in this
white paper stem from his expertise in the areas of diversity in children's materials and library programming for diverse populations. He authored this paper
based upon this expertise and not as a representative of ALSC.

CLAUDIA HAINES
nevershushed.com

Evaluating Apps and New Media for Young Children: A Rubric

The rubric is divided into two parts:

- The technical/user experience criteria for both story and toy apps (Part 1)
- The additional content criteria specific to either story apps *or* toy apps (Part 2)

Award one point for each question answered with a yes. There are 22 questions for each app if both parts of the rubric are considered. A perfect score is ideal—for example, 11/11 technical elements and 11/11 content elements—but some apps may not get a perfect score and still have a valuable place in a program or a child's learning experience.

PART 1

Story and Toy Apps

Both story (book) apps and toy (game) apps should be evaluated according to several similar technical and user experience criteria. *About all apps, librarians and caregivers should ask these eleven questions.*

Yes (1)	No (0)	11 Elements Found in High-Quality Story *and* Toy Apps (Technical/User Experience)
		1. Is the app's navigation clear for the intended audience? Does it have intuitive way-finding?
		2. Does the app work free of glitches?
		3. Do sound effects, if included, enhance the app experience? Are there settings for turning on/off music and other sound effects, if they are not crucial to the story or play?
		4. Does the app feature a clean, uncluttered display?
		5. Is the necessary equipment available to offer a positive experience? For example, is a large monitor needed to best view the app? Or is the tablet screen appropriate? Does the app require additional physical hardware?
		6. Is the app free of links to social media and the Internet? If not, can access be disabled in the app or device settings?
		7. Does the app developer state it will *not* collect data about you or your child within the app?
		8. Are there developmentally appropriate cues for interactivity?
		9. Are there parental tips, restrictions, and settings within the app and/or within the device's settings to customize the child(ren)'s experience?
		10. Do the app's technical features encourage joint media engagement?
		11. Is the app free of in-app purchases or in-app ads? If not, are they easily ignored and hard to access by young children? For example, can in-app purchases be disabled in the device settings? Can a password be required for in-app purchases?

PART 2A

Story Apps

Story, or book, apps have unique content and provide specific user experiences. Some of the qualities are similar to those found in high-quality children's picture books, while some are specific to the digital format. Many book apps are, in fact, print books transformed for the digital environment. *When evaluating story apps, consider these additional eleven questions.*

Yes (1)	No (0)	11 Elements Found in High-Quality Story Apps (Content)
		1. Does the app feature a great story with high-quality images and a narrative that entices the reader to read again and again? (Repetition deepens a young reader's understanding of the story.)
		2. Is the story original or is it a previously published story that is *strongly enhanced* in the digital form?
		3. Does the app include accurate information and grammatically correct content?
		4. Are the story's characters culturally and ethnically diverse and include experiences that reflect today's diverse families?
		5. Is the content appropriate for the targeted age group?
		6. Are opportunities to strengthen the Every Child Ready to Read early literacy skills, where appropriate, included?
		7. Does the app include meaningful interactive elements that maintain the story's flow and add to the story instead of being only for interactivity's sake? (Elements should engage the reader and should help the reader better understand the content instead of distract from the story.)
		8. Is the font plain and highly readable, both of which are beneficial for the learning reader and for groups who are experiencing the app on either a small or big screen?
		9. Are read-to-me and read-to-myself options available, allowing families to read and listen together? (Narration should be well spoken and expressive.)
		10. Does the app include multiple language options and a voice record option to foster literacy in home languages?
		11. Does the app's content encourage joint media engagement?

PART 2B

Toy/Creation Apps

Toy apps, also known as game or creation apps, include activities, puzzles, and/or games, usually without the narrative found in a story app. Along with the technical and user experience features mentioned above, *consider these eleven important elements specific to toy apps.*

Yes (1)	No (0)	11 Elements Found in High-Quality Toy Apps (Content)
		1. Does the app offer open-ended play?
		2. Does the app's content encourage joint media engagement and collaboration?
		3. Do the activities, games, or puzzles foster creativity?
		4. Is the content appropriate for the targeted age group?
		5. Does the app strengthen one or more of the Every Child Ready to Read early literacy practices, where appropriate?
		6. Are the activities, puzzles, or games customizable depending on the child's interest and experience?
		7. Is the app sufficiently engaging to warrant multiple uses?
		8. Are the app's concepts presented clearly?
		9. Does the app reflect diverse users by including culturally and ethnically diverse characters, environments, and experiences?
		10. Are STEM/STEAM concepts addressed?
		11. Are the images and/or graphic details high quality?

Bibliography

ALA Think Tank. www.facebook.com/groups/ALAthinkTANK/search/?query=alsc%20 white%20paper.

Alper, Meryl. *Digital Youth with Disabilities.* Cambridge: MIT Press, 2014. https:// mitpress.mit.edu/books/digital-youth-disabilities.

ALSC Education Committee. *Competencies for Librarians Serving Children in Public Libraries.* Chicago: Association for Library Service to Children, 2015.

American Academy of Pediatrics. *Policy Statement: Children, Adolescents, and the Media.* http://pediatrics.aappublications.org/content/132/5/958.full.

American Library Association. "Core Values of Librarianship." www.ala.org/advocacy/ intfreedom/statementspols/corevalues.

———. Reference and User Services Association. "Guidelines for Behavioral Performance of Reference and Information Service Providers." www.ala.org/ rusa/resources/guidelines/guidelinesbehavioral.

Armstrong, Amanda. "Discussions about Diversity at ISTE2015." *Uncomfortable Conversations for Educators and Parents* (blog). http://uncomfortableconversa tions4educators.com/2015/07/05/discussions-about-diversity-at-iste2015/.

Brown, Ari, Donald A. Shifrin, and David I. Hill. "Beyond 'Turn It Off': How to Advise Families on Media Use." *AAP News* 36. October 2015. www.aappublications.org/content/36/10/54.

Campbell, Cen, Claudia Haines, Amy Koester, and Dorothy Stoltz. *Media Mentorship for Libraries Serving Youth.* Chicago: Association for Library Service to Children, 2015.

Dresang, Eliza T. "How the iPad Affects Young Children, and What We Can Do about It." Filmed 2013. TEDxMidAtlantic video, 13:14. Posted April 2014. http://tedxtalks.ted.com/video/How-the-iPad-affects-young-child.

———. *Radical Change: Books for Youth in a Digital Age.* New York: H. W. Wilson, 1999.

———. *Screen Time: How Electronic Media—From Baby Videos to Educational Software—Affects Your Young Child.* New York: Basic Books, 2012.

Guernsey Lisa, and Michael Levine. *Tap, Click, Read: Growing Readers in a World of Screens.* San Francisco: Jossey-Bass, 2015.

Guernsey, Lisa, et al. *Pioneering Literacy in the Digital Wild West.* Campaign for Grade-Level Reading. 2012. http://gradelevelreading.net/wp-content/uploads/2012/12/GLR_TechnologyGuide_final.pdf.

Im, Janice H., et al. *Cradling Literacy: Building Teachers' Skills to Nurture Early Language and Literacy Birth to Five.* Washington, DC: Zero to Three, 2007. http://main.zerotothree.org/site/PageServer?pagename=ter_key_language_importance.

"iPad in Education." Apple. www.apple.com/education/ipad/apps-books-and-more/.

Jenkins, Henry. "*Tap, Click, Read: An Interview with Lisa Guernsey and Michael Levine* (Part Three)." October 27, 2015. http://henryjenkins.org/2015/10/tap-click-read-an-interview-with-lisa-guernsey-and-michael-levine-part-three.html.

Jonassen, Wendi, and Ryan Loughlin. "A 17th-Century Russian Community Living in 21st-Century Alaska." *The Atlantic.* May 1, 2013. www.theatlantic.com/national/archive/2013/05/a-17th-century-russian-community-living-in-21st-century-alaska/275440/.

Kabali, H. K., et al. "Exposure and Use of Mobile Media Devices by Young Children." *Pediatrics* 136, no. 6 (February 2015): 1044–50. http://pediatrics.aappublications.org/content/early/2015/10/28/peds.2015-2151.

Kluver, Carisa. "Parenting in the Digital Age: Teaching Kids to Balance Their Own Media Diet." *The Digital Media Diet* (blog). March 7, 2014. http://digitalmediadiet.com/parenting-in-the-digital-age-teaching-kids-to-balance-their-own-media-diet/.

———. "What Is a Digital Media Diet?" *The Digital Media Diet* (blog). http://digitalmediadiet.com/what-is-a-digital-media-diet/.

Leckart, Steven. "Balance Your Media Diet." *Wired.* July 15, 2009. www.wired.com/2009/07/by-media-diet/.

Levinson, A. M., et al. *Diverse Families and Media: Using Research to Inspire Design*. New York: The Joan Ganz Cooney Center at Sesame Workshop, 2015.

"MLS Specializations: Youth Experience (YX)." University of Maryland College of Information Studies. http://ischool.umd.edu/mls_specializations#YX.

NAEYC, and Fred Rogers Center. *Technology and Interactive Media as Tools in Early Childhood Programs Serving Children from Birth through Age 8*. www.naeyc.org/files/naeyc/file/positions/PS_technology_WEB2.pdf.

Naidoo, Jamie Campbell. *The Importance of Diversity in Library Programs and Material Collections for Children*. Chicago: Association for Library Service to Children, 2014.

Naidoo, Jamie Campbell, and Sarah Park Dahlen. *Diversity Programming for Digital Youth: Promoting Cultural Competence in the Children's Library*. Santa Barbara, CA: Libraries Unlimited, 2014.

National Teen Lock-in. https://sites.google.com/site/teenlibrarylockin/home.

Nelson, Jennifer, and Keith Braafladt. *Technology and Literacy: 21st Century Library Programming for Children and Teens*. Chicago: American Library Association, 2012.

Parrott, Kiera. "Circulating iPads in the Children's Library." *ALSC Blog*. November 15, 2011. www.alsc.ala.org/blog/2011/11/circulating-ipads-in-the-childrens-library/.

Prensky, Marc. *From Digital Natives to Digital Wisdom*. Thousand Oaks, CA: Corwin, 2012.

Reddy, Sumathi. "Pediatricians Rethink Screen Time Policy." *Wall Street Journal*. October 12, 2015. www.wsj.com/articles/pediatricians-rethink-screen-time-policy-for-children-1444671636.

Rideout, Vicky. *The Common Sense Census: Media Use by Tweens and Teens*. San Francisco: Common Sense Media, 2015. https://www.commonsensemedia.org/sites/default/files/uploads/research/census_researchreport.pdf.

Ryan, Camille. *Language Use in the United States: 2011*. American Community Survey Reports. Washington, DC: U.S. Census Bureau, August 2013. https://www.census.gov/prod/2013pubs/acs-22.pdf.

Samuel, Alexandra. "Parents: Reject Technology Shame." *The Atlantic*. November 4, 2015. http://www.theatlantic.com/technology/archive/2015/11/why-parents-shouldnt-feel-technology-shame/414163/.

———. "What Kind of Digital Parent Are You?" *@Alexandra Samuel* (blog). November 12, 2015. http://alexandrasamuel.com/parenting/what-kind-of-digital-parent-are-you.

Shifrin, Donald A., et al. *Growing Up Digital: Media Research Symposium*. American Academy of Pediatrics. Rosemont, IL, May 2–3, 2015, 1. https://www.aap.org/en-us/documents/digital_media_symposium_proceedings.pdf.

Takeuchi, Lori, and Reed Stevens. *The New Coviewing: Designing for Learning through Joint Media Engagement.* New York: The Joan Ganz Cooney Center, 2011. www.joanganzcooneycenter.org/wp-content/uploads/2011/12/jgc_coviewing_desktop.pdf.

Vaala, Sarah. "New Stakes in the Market: A Researcher and New Parent 'Gets a Read on' the App Stores." *Ed Central* (blog). December 9, 2015. www.edcentral.org/get-a-read-on-apps/?utm_source=NCFL+Literacy+NOW&utm_campaign=f8d923264f-11_6_15&utm_medium=email&utm_term=0_ddbeaff477-f8d923264f-67117105.

Whitby, Tom. "How Do I Get a PLN?" *Edutopia* (blog). November 18, 2013. www.edutopia.org/blog/how-do-i-get-a-pln-tom-whitby.

Zero to Eight: Children's Media Use in America 2013 Infographic. San Francisco: Common Sense Media, 2013. www.commonsensemedia.org/zero-to-eight-2013-infographic.

Index